From Myth to Belief

Copyright © 2012 Greeks for Christ / Orama Publications
Box 6536, Oakland, CA 94603, USA
e-mail: orders@greeksforchrist.org
www.greeksforchrist.org

All rights reserved. No part of this publication may be translated, reproduced, broadcast, performed in any form, or transmitted in any form or by any means, electronic or mechanical, including photocopying and recording, or by any information storage and retrieval system, without the written permission of the Publisher, except brief extracts by a reviewer for inclusion in critical articles or reviews.

Printed in the United States of America. All trademarks are owned by their respective companies.

Produced as a service of Simple Publishing.
www.simplepublishing.com

For my parents, the late
Nikos and Rosa Vourliotis,
who taught me to think freely and to respect God.

Theo N. Vourliotis was born in Athens, Greece. He studied Political Science and Business in Greece and California. He immigrated to the San Francisco Bay Area in 1975.

He has written many articles in newspapers and magazines of the Greek Diaspora. His book *Ellinas Forever* (Greek) has become a hit among Greeks in the US. He has been co-producer of *The Greek Hour of Hope* radio broadcast and Greek language editor of the bilingual magazine *Chrisma* since 1975.

He is married to Sofie Anastasiadou and now lives in Greece for most of the year.

The heroes in this book have shared their life's story with Theo, and he knows each one of them personally.

At this point in time, everyone mentioned in this book is a firm believer and leads a Christian life which glorifies God and is beneficial to others.

From Myth to Belief
Twenty-two Amazing Accounts of Changed Lives

The entertainment of Greek myths is well documented. Sixth century BC fabulist Aesop and his fictitious legends have become world famous. His readers' acquaintance with myths prompted the Apostle Peter to assure them, "We did not follow cleverly devised myths when we made known to you the power and coming of our Lord Jesus Christ, but we were eyewitnesses of his majesty" (2 Peter 1:16 RSV).

The marvelous stories published in From Myth to Belief are similarly true, documented, accounts of people from all walks of life who have experienced the transforming power of God through faith in Jesus Christ.

For more than thirty-five years, I have been privileged to observe great miracles in folks who put their trust in the Lord Jesus Christ, "Who by the power at work within us is able to do far more abundantly than all that we ask or think" (Ephesians 3:20 Nestle-Aland).

Like Peter and the other two disciples who saw Christ transformed "on the holy mountain," my colleagues and I at Greeks for Christ International and the Greek Assembly have been changed forever by the miracles we have witnessed through the years. Each true story proves the gospel to be not futile theory, but authoritative truth. God's foes who became his faithful servants, the incarcerated who found liberty in Christ, the incurable who recovered and the broken families that reunited offer an undeniable witness to God's power.

Witnessing the glorious Christ was no myth for the apostles, but a life-changing experience. The apostle John wrote, "we saw His glory" (John 1:14), and Peter added "we heard (God's) voice from heaven" and "we were with Him on the holy mountain" (2 Peter 1:18). While the apostolic witness stands alone, the stories here are living examples of those who saw, heard, and lived the glory and the power of God in our time.

And, as Transfiguration fulfilled biblical prophesy and "the prophetic word was confirmed" (2 Peter 1:19), the experiences in the book attest the Bible as God's Word. The Bible is not a collection of myths, as some have advocated, or a mere book on the same level as all the others. Instead, we are told in 2 Peter 1:19 that "you will do well to pay attention to this (God's Word) as to a lamp shining in a dark place." The entire Bible is divinely inspired and without error in its original form.

As you read these pages, I trust you will be encouraged

to believe, opening your heart to Jesus Christ to learn what God has for you, and asking Him to meet your need. And, if you have not invited Jesus as your Savior and Lord, I would admonish you to do so now. For, it is our desire at Greeks for Christ to present the gospel in the power of the Holy Spirit that people will put their trust in God, accept Christ as their Savior, and serve Him in the fellowship of His Church.

Dr. Peter Vourliotis
Oakland, California

Table of Contents

The Transforming Power of Christ   13

    The Miracle of May   16
    God Loves Those Who Hate Him   25
    From an Anarchist Atheist
       to a Useful Christian   38
    I Don't Want to Die!   47
    What Should I Do to Become
       a Good Christian?   55

Changes in Prisoner's Lives   60

    Dangerous Dan   64
    Life from Death Row   74
    A Last Wish   90

Miracles of Healing   95

    Recreating my Face   99
    Without the Fear of Death   110
    Medicine for Cancer   125

Table of Contents

Restoration of Families   129

    Can a Broken Family Reunite?   132
    The Claim Letter that was
       Never Delivered   139
    Something Wonderful will
       Happen to You!   149
    The World Champion Who
       was "Resurrected"   157
    Now You're a Christian!   164

Stories of Lives Changed   184

    A Lifelong Adventure   187
    One Day All Will be Well...   195
    How Often Do You Read the Bible?   208
    I'm Walkin', Folks...It's a Miracle!   214
    A Miracle Like No Other...   223
    Which Religion is the Best?   229

The Transforming Power of Christ

I'm a survivor. No, I didn't win a million dollars by outplaying, outlasting and outwitting contestants on a reality TV show. Two decades ago, I survived a different jungle: clinical depression. But the power of the risen Christ rescued me from emotional death.

My pastoral ministry in Northern California was thriving. Attendance was up. Complaints were down. Then, without warning, I lost my balance and fell into a dark emotional basement. Years of workaholic tendencies led me to the top of the stairs, but a couple of unexpected events tripped me up. I discovered an irreconcilable conflict with a staff member, and my father nearly died from a massive heart attack. Each morning when I looked into the mirror, I was reminded of my own mortality and imperfection.

It was more than I could handle. One day life seemed meaningless. The next day I felt the same. I was continuously sad. No matter how I tried, I couldn't concentrate for any length of time. I saw the blue sky and green hills surrounding the church as black and white (mostly black). The sound of my ringing telephone drove me to the edge.

I'll never forget the emotional paralysis I felt standing before the congregation on Easter Sunday 1990. They were expecting good news about the power of the living Christ made possible by the empty tomb. As far as I was concerned, it was still Good Friday. I felt like a hypocrite.

My superintendent recommended a sabbatical, but the church board said it wasn't feasible financially. Ministry had to continue. But how could it? I was spiritually bankrupt. I was empty and powerless. But then I discovered the transformative power of the Holy Spirit in amazing ways.

Like King David, who faced his own dark night of the soul, I discovered the Lord could shepherd me through the chilly dark valley of death's shadows. In spite of my inner pain, I called out to God with sighs and groans. Over a series of months, the black clouds of despair lifted. The joy of my salvation returned. The following Easter I stood before my flock attesting to the fact that the Spirit who raised Jesus from the dead had empowered my mortal body also.

It has been nearly twenty years since my nine-month bout with depression. Interestingly, I can say that my life is richer for the experience. No, I didn't win a million dollars or become a television celebrity. But I did survive. And in the process I tasted flavors of God's grace and gained understanding of my own limits — limits I previously didn't know existed. Yes, the power of God can change lives.

Greg Asimakoupoulos
Seattle, Washington

Greg Asimakoupoulos holds a Bachelor of Arts in Biblical Literature from Seattle Pacific University and a Master of Divinity from North Park Theological Seminary. Greg is the author of ten books and more than 300 magazine articles. His weekly blog Rhymes and Reasons can be accessed at www.partialobserver.com. Greg and his wife Wendy have been married for twenty-six years and have three daughters.

The Miracle of May

*There is no way you face heaven
and remain unmoved.*

I was twelve the first time the heavens opened in front of my very eyes, as I peered through a telescope in the observatory in my hometown. All the mythical worlds of heroes, of demigods and of angels I had heard stories of as a small child suddenly became a real world that I could, say, touch with my own hands. My joy was indescribable, my fantasy rode wild, and my desire became a decision. I ran home and announced it enthusiastically to my parents.

"I will become an astronomer!"

When I was a little girl, I went to Sunday school and church with neighborhood kids. I liked it. One of those Sundays, I asked the Sunday school teacher whether stories about interplanetary travel – man going to the moon and stars – if all this would ever become reality. She replied laconically,

"If God wanted man in space, He would have put him up there himself."

This answer not only disappointed me, but it has kept me away from both Sunday school and church ever since.

I went to a school with an emphasis on science and then studied astronomy at the University of California at Berkeley. There I met a wonderful Greek born in Egypt named Spyros. Spyros introduced me to Greek culture,

The Miracle of May

which I loved deeply.

Even after many years of friendship, he still plays an important role in my life.

When I met Spyros, God was a minor factor in my life. My science, I thought, made the biblical stories that I learned as a child completely false, if not laughable. After my graduation from Berkeley, because I loved Spyros' family, Greece and her culture, I moved and taught in Greece. In a few years I met the love of my life, and I got married to a Greek.

Our wedding took place on May 1st with all the grandeur of the Greek Orthodox Church and the magic of spring. A year later, on May 13th, the joy of our life came to the world: a beautiful, perfect little girl we named Sophia. Even after this miracle, I could not find even a small place in my heart for God. When Sophia was five years old, she fell ill, and doctors discovered that she suffered from two active-chronic illnesses. Our world was suddenly shattered. Immediately, I took my baby to Boston for better diagnosis and treatment and then returned to Greece. When Sophia turned eleven, it became apparent that she was too ill to remain in Greece. I took her to the San Francisco Bay Area, so she could have the best treatment in the world at the University Clinics in Stanford, San Francisco, and the other hospitals in this highly developed region of America. While my family was back in California, we were able to reconnect with Spyros and his family.

Over the next ten years, our live changed drastically. It indeed became hell, but still remained a paradise. Sophia suffered terribly. There were frequent visits to hospitals, accompanied by many surgeries, medication and daily

From Myth to Belief

injections. The doctors continually monitored Sophia, and I provided a mother's ever-watchful eye. Despite this, Sophia remained the most fearless creature I've ever met in my life. Her style was classy, her face serene and beautiful, and her angelic singing voice resounded with power and sweetness. She had a wonderful voice. Her personality was strong, coupled with a million dollar attitude. She would enter a company of people she did not know, and immediately they all wanted to be her friends. She loved everyone, and she affected everyone around her positively. She faced everything with a smile, as if nothing was happening. Where did she find all this power? Never could I understand.

Plenty of love from me and her father and relatives and friends always surrounded Sophia. I had certainly never looked up nor invited God to help us although Spyros, who is a strong Christian, often talked to me about God. Over those ten years of trials and tribulations, Spyros and his family, who had re-entered our lives since we returned to San Francisco, turned out to be the most loyal friends being always present to support us. Nonetheless, whenever Spyros tried to talk to me about God, I cut him off. He, however, was patient with us. And he was praying for us.

From a very, very young age, Sophia set goals in her life and methodically worked towards achieving them. One of the goals she set was to become an actress-singer. She was just a little girl when she began receiving important roles in school projects, as well as in recitals. Later in college she majored in drama and music.

On May 13, 1995, Sophia turned twenty-one years old. She was a real beauty. That night, we went to San

The Miracle of May

Francisco for a double celebration; for her birthday and for securing the lead role in a play in a professional theater of the San Francisco Bay Area. Our joy was indescribable. Sophia's dream had become reality. The performances, which began in the middle of that month, were crowned with great success. The actors were excellent. The talent of actress Sophia Eugenia, her artistic name, was awesome. The reviews were wonderful. My daughter, my pride, Francisco Bay Area. I felt inexpressible joy mixed with pride that only a parent can feel for her child. In two weeks, the play was over as planned.

That same evening, however, something else was also over. I do not exactly know what happened to my Sophia on that fateful night, but I remember she was rushed to the Medical Clinic of Stanford University. The doctors took her immediately to the emergency room and with tremendous effort did everything possible to save her life. I found myself outside the room – with Spyros. Once the doctors allowed us to see her, Spyros immediately went and sat very close to her so that she could hear him well. He leaned over and talked to her in Greek about Jesus for some time. He assured her of His love and urged her to fear nothing, because "He would be with her whatever happened." Later Spyros told me that he was confident in his heart that Sophia had heard and understood everything he told her. Then we had to go back and stay in the hallway. Spyros immediately shut himself in a room and continued to pray. I stood at one end of the hallway looking at the revolving doors at the other end.

Suddenly, I saw my mother, who had died fifteen years

From Myth to Belief

before. I saw her standing near the revolving doors with hands outstretched to Sophia, as if inviting her. And I saw Sophia with arms outstretched to her grandmother and ready to leave. They were both so very beautiful and radiant that it took my breath away. I do not know how long the vision lasted, but I realized I was allowed to see them together because I could trust my daughter only with my mother. How well God knew me! But even then I did not allow Him entry into my life. Even then I didn't understand His plans.

What had happened? I refused to accept that the last scene had concluded and the curtain had fallen on the most bitter, yet the sweetest drama of the last sixteen years. I sat alone in the middle of the theater, waiting impatiently for my heroine to get out on stage and continue performing. But in vain. The heroine, my daughter, was not coming. Thus, in the early hours of May 31st, Sophia's life also ended suddenly, without any warning. As the theater lights shut off, so did the spotlight of my life extinguish. My reason to live was abruptly uprooted. My Sophia was snatched out of my arms.

I asked Spyros to find a priest who would not mix gods and mortals at a funeral.

He told me, "Well, I know a priest, but he is a good man. He will say exactly the right things for the occasion."

Because I had no choice, I accepted. Sophia's funeral was conducted by Dr. Peter, who spoke in English and in Greek for all to understand.

Sophia's funeral was a huge surprise to me. I expected to attend an ordinary, tearful funeral service. Instead, I

The Miracle of May

heard words of hope like I had never heard before in my life; a sermon that I wished never ended. At that moment, I knew exactly where my daughter had gone, yet I could not fully fathom how God was working in my life. I felt that important things were happening within me, but I didn't understand them. A few days later, I had an exceptional dream. Sophia came to me and said, "Don't worry, Mommy. I'm fine here. I'm working with Him. I'm singing!"

The next Sunday, I asked Spyros to take me to the church where Dr. Peter preached, because I craved to hear those words of hope again. He preached about the love of Christ, who came into this world to be crucified for the sins of men whose man's disregard for God has made him unhappy. At the end of the sermon, with tearful eyes, I received this love of Christ in my life.

Suddenly, in the moment of my salvation, my spirit and my mind and my heart and my soul opened. I realized just who the "Him" was that my daughter had mentioned in the dream. That's when I understood and accepted the "Him" who created the firmament and all those worlds which I observed and taught. I knew the Creator of the earth and sky of my science was also full of infinite love, ready to save the heart of every person as soon as they asked for Him. My intellect opened to understand that in the same way God is able to rule the universe perfectly, so is He able to rule perfectly the life of every human being, including my own if I allowed him. So, I opened myself to Him and surrendered completely. I opened my heart for God to enter! And I did it consciously. Now I was not only a scientist who had knowledge of the laws of heavens

From Myth to Belief

with mathematical precision. I was one who had exact knowledge, for I had met the Creator of heaven and earth including myself. And now not only God but also all the people around me at the church enveloped me with love and consolation.

Sometime after all this, I found this wonderful poem:

A Child Loaned
"I'll lend you for a little time
a child of mine", He said,
"For you to love the while she lives,
and mourn for when she's dead.

She may be six or seven years,
or even twenty-one or three,
But will you, till I call her back,
take care of her for me?

She'll bring her charm to gladden you,
and, should her stay be brief,
You'll have her lovely memories
as solace for your grief.

I cannot promise she will stay,
since all from earth return,
But there are lessons taught down there
I want this child to learn.

I've looked the wide world over
in my search for teachers true

The Miracle of May

And from the throng that crowd life's lanes
I have selected you.

Now will you give her all your love,
nor think the labor's vain,
Nor hate me when I come to call
and take her back again?"

I fancied that I heard them say,
"Dear Lord, thy will be done,
For all the joys thy child shall bring
the risk of grief we'll run.

We'll shelter her with tenderness,
we'll love her while we may
And for the happiness we've known
for ever grateful stay.

But, should the angels call for her
much sooner than we'd planned
We'll brave the bitter grief that comes
and try to understand."

I returned to my husband in Greece in October of that same year. Since then, I've been involved in the church of my parish. Besides being the pianist, I take courses at St. John College of Theology of England.

I look back and see how God has guided the steps of our family for the better, regardless of whether we have felt or understood it. We have missed the love of Sophia,

From Myth to Belief

but I can say I truly feel the tangible, infinite love of God replenishing me in excess. Some skeptics will argue that my intellect, as a safeguard, played a trick on me. It has caused me to escape into an alternate reality because the present one is unbearable to me.

But faith was born inside of me after I heard the pure Word of God for the first time. This experience is undeniable.

I can still say that the temporary death of my beloved daughter makes me feel like a parent at a very, very small, but distinct way, the pain the heart of Father God, the parent, felt when he saw his Son dying on Calvary temporarily. At the end of every day, I thank God for the depth of His wisdom and for keeping my Sophia safe in His arms until I go there to see her again, to be together forever in a world beyond tears, pain and sorrow that He has prepared for us. A world described in His Word; a world much more beautiful than the one that I have studied through science; A glorious world that "no eye has seen, no ear has heard, no mind has ever conceived" (1 Corinthians 2:9), one that even the strongest atomic telescope on Earth or in space has caught. A perfect world, whose source of energy, never-ending light, and life eternal is His glory. I also thank the Holy Spirit for His peace and consolation, which He continues to give me, and for putting words in my mouth and words to my pen when I need to tell the story of my life and the miracle of May.

Concord, California; Athens, Greece
As I heard the story from Sherry Angelis

God Loves Those Who Hate Him

The cycle of child abuse can be broken only by something stronger than violence.

"Christians! Dumb, worthless people, who have been brainwashed, abdicated personal responsibility and clung in desperation and ignorance to their imaginary God-crutch; 'holier than thou,' self-righteous bigots whose sole aim is to force their stifling, judgmental, and immoral morality on the rest of us." These are gentle words compared to the hostile, profanity-laced vitriol I used during my childhood and young adult life as an atheist.

When I was a university student, I once walked into the student center and encountered a young man in the open walkway talking about Jesus and inviting students to a meeting. With undisguised contempt, I told him I didn't believe in God. He said, with a pleading look on his face (which made me think he was even dumber than I originally supposed), "May I ask why?"

"Because I think it is an excuse for not using one's mind and taking responsibility for one's own actions and life," I responded.

Earnestly he said, "Oh, if you only knew!" I rolled my eyes, shook my head in supercilious disgust and made a quick exit to avoid being subjected to what I considered an

From Myth to Belief

inane, idiotic lack of logic.

Whether I started my life with such hatred, I'm not sure. I'm pretty sure I didn't start out as an atheist. If I go far enough back in my memory, I vaguely remember a small child who believed and trusted that there was a God. I don't know if I was taught this in Sunday school at the church my family sometimes attended at the urging of my mother. Perhaps I accepted it from the simple prayer we recited before dinner: "God is good, God is great, let us thank Him for our food. Amen." Or perhaps I heard God mentioned when our family attended sunrise Easter services at Punchbowl National Cemetery: I can remember rising excitedly before dawn, my father and brother donning aloha shirts, dress slacks and covered shoes, my mother and sister wearing powder blue or bright yellow dresses, and I, an irritating, lace-trimmed one that made me itch.

Vaguely I can remember crying out to this God from beneath my sheets at night, pleading for the pain I felt to go away or, better, to be taken out of my home. I think perhaps on a few occasions I asked to die. On the one hand, I remember a mother who was loving, sweet, patient and not easily angered. On the other, unfortunately, I remember a father who, as it seemed to a child – me – easily moved to tears, often exploded in anger and lashed out verbally, physically and emotionally.

My father was very well educated, he was a dentist surgeon. He had also loved beauty: art, photography, music, culture. When he and his fellow Japanese-American soldiers of the 442nd were on leave in Europe during WWII, my father chose to visit a famous opera house and other places of artistic or cultural interest, unlike his buddies.

God Loves Those Who Hate Him

During his lifetime, he bought paintings, sculptures and curios that, while not expensive, delighted his fancy; he also frequented pawn shops for unique collectibles and owned several rare art books. He listened to classical music with the sound turned up so high that it seemed he wished to lose himself in the chords. It was, therefore, a big question to me, how an important person like him would mistreat *me*, his own child?

I was unable to fully appreciate the breathtaking beauty of the Hawaiian beaches and sunshine that surrounded me because my own personal world was overshadowed by an overwhelming feeling of chaos and confusion, of explosions about to happen or just having happened, and of seemingly irremediable pain.

I prayed, and I got no response. And so, by the age of perhaps nine or ten, having experienced too much personal injustice and having received no response for its remedy, I reasoned that:

(a) If God existed, then He would be loving and kind and would not want me to suffer abuse;

(b) I continued to suffer abuse – God did not remove me from that household; and

(c) therefore, God must not exist.

There is a rule of inference in philosophy called "Modus Tolens," which says: If P, then Q. Not Q; therefore, not P. In this case, P is the statement "God exists" and Q is the statement "God is loving and kind, and does not want children to suffer abuse." If one concludes "not Q," that is, it is not the case that God is loving and kind and doesn't want children to suffer abuse, then one must conclude "not P," that it is not the case that God exists.

From Myth to Belief

I reasoned according to reality as I understood it. It took twenty more years for me to find that both P and Q were true. God exists, and He is loving and kind and does not want children to suffer abuse. However, there was much I had to learn about the complexities of Q. I had to learn His love and kindness and how He revealed these to people. Everything I learned about God would defy my own human reasoning.

I learned later that God did not avert His eyes when I was being abused. He saw, and it grieved Him. It grieved Him to see me being hit and kicked, and told the soul-murdering words, "You should never have been born," "You were a mistake," or "You're a worthless." I learned also that God's heart ached for my father, for the pain in my father's heart. Yet, God did not intervene, and it made no sense to me.

I grew up, became more logical (or so I thought) and more depressed. Yet, I believed that there must be an absolute truth, and I searched for it. I moved to the East Coast to attend graduate school for philosophy, but found no truth, only ways to determine fallacies in the logical structure of one's reasoning. I dropped out after the first semester. Logic is not truth; it is merely structure, without substance. I dabbled in Zen Buddhism, spent hours counting my breaths from one to ten and back again, and meditating on one nonsensical word, and found no truth and no lasting peace.

The Bible says, "...you will seek the Lord your God, and you will find Him if you seek Him with all your heart and with all your soul" (Deuteronomy 4:29). Jesus says, "I am the way, the truth and the life. No one comes to the Father

God Loves Those Who Hate Him

except through Me" (John. 14:6). The Word also says, "And you shall know the truth, and the truth shall make you free" (John 8:32). I really wanted to *know* "The Truth."

I moved from Massachusetts to Northern California, experienced a few more painful personal circumstances, and found myself wanting to believe in God. It frustrated me that I could not. I continued to reason that it made no sense to me to believe in a God for Whom I saw no empirical evidence.

I studied popular psychology. One evening, I conducted a psychological exercise on myself, asking myself question after question, leading to more questions. I felt myself going logically further and further. Suddenly, I came to the reasoned, not emotional, conclusion that ultimately, logically, given what I believed, (including that I had come into being on this earth having evolved over millions of years by accident from a single cell into a human being), there was no reason for my existence. There was no reason that I should exist.

My existence or my nonexistence had the same value. I also concluded that there was no purpose for my existence. The fact that I sat there thinking and breathing was a mystery. I had liked to believe that there was a reason for everything, to make sense out of things. Now, I found that my existence simply didn't make sense. Please understand that I was not at all suicidal; I was logical, and this was a logical conclusion.

As if in a vision, I felt myself falling into an abyss. It was deep, dark and unending. Terrified by the feeling of falling, I cried out in my mind for help — to whom, I did not know. I simply exclaimed, "HELP ME!" Unbelievably, in the next

From Myth to Belief

instant, I simply knew, without a doubt, that there was a God, and that His essence was Love and Goodness. It makes no sense, but it was as if a mental wave of love washed over me. It was as if I felt His love lift me out of the abyss. Then, a voice told me, "Look for the good, and when you find it, hold onto it and never let it go." And then I heard (which made no sense at the time), "He's very beautiful." God saw me in my wretched though hungry state and was merciful to me.

God was not an idea of my own wishful thinking. I had wished before, but was met by silence. Now, however, I had experienced His love. I knew that He existed and no one could tell me otherwise. I knew His goodness. I discovered that God was not an idea in my mind, but a real entity to be experienced. Because I had experienced Him personally, I began to watch Christian TV programs and listen to Christian radio teachers. I followed their suggestion to receive Christ into my life and ask forgiveness for my sins. Unfortunately, I was still operating in the intellectual realm. Christ only made sense to me as an abstract concept, not as a real person, and I did not think that I was particularly sinful. I was, I maintained, a victim. Yet, as I searched for "the good," I continued to feel God's loving presence.

The Bible says, "I drew them with gentle cords, with bands of love, and I was to them as those who take the yoke from their neck. I stooped and fed them" (Hosea 11:4). My father had stood over me with a belt or a hanger and beaten me. God, however, was stooping in humility to my level, with open arms, and lovingly feeding my soul. He was defying my logic and preconceptions. As I chased after Him, I felt I needed to make changes in my life, which

God Loves Those Who Hate Him

I gladly did, breaking detrimental personal relationships. I made a list of things I wanted (including the type of living space and job I wanted), and watched in amazement as those requests were answered.

Ultimately, I met someone who urged me to go to his church. He encouraged me while enduring my profanity and pointed attacks on his character. I could hardly believe I was keeping company with a "born-again" Christian. I had thought all born-again Christians were evil, judgmental, self-righteous bigots. Yet, contrary to my preconceptions, I felt there was something special about this person and his experience of God, so I went to his church with him. Once there, I was amazed that everyone was so happy.

On a certain Sunday in that church, I felt as if the preacher was speaking directly to me. Not preaching against me, but speaking directly to my heart. He said, "You who believe that God is good, loving and kind, how do you know? The only way we know is because He came to earth and showed us in the person of Jesus Christ." Those words gripped me. "How do I know God is good?" I thought. "How do I know He's loving?" For the first time I nervously thought, "What if I've been wrong?" I had believed that Jesus was just a man, and an arrogant man at that, claiming to be God. Now, I felt as if time and fate were moving at an accelerated pace. The "what if" began to evolve into, "Oh, no. I think I've been wrong!"

One of the things on my wish list that God had granted was to live in a house on a hill, with lots of trees and yet lots of sunshine. I had found such a property owned by a businesswoman who rented out several rooms in her large house high in the hills of Oakland, isolated from other

From Myth to Belief

homes and surrounded by forest land. Unfortunately, the area's isolation attracted criminal activity.

Just a few days later, with the thought, "I think I've been wrong," fresh in my mind, a woman was shot in the head and left to die in the street a few yards from the house. Alerted by a passing motorist, my housemates and I came outside. I stooped next to her body and prayed to God to let her live.

The next day, I called the police and was excited to receive the news that the injured woman was alive and had identified her attacker. My born-again Christian friend and I went out to dinner to celebrate the good news.

However, on the way home that night, I encountered on the side of the old frontage road a naked female corpse. As I frantically drove past the body, I suddenly heard a deep, loud, long, sinister laugh, which I knew immediately was the devil.

Up until that moment, I had believed that there was no devil, that the reason people did terrible things was that they had been raised under terrible, inhumane conditions that had taught them to do terrible, inhumane things. For the first time, I knew how it felt to have chills go down one's spine. And, I knew I was not safe sitting on my spiritual fence. I had to choose to accept or reject Christ forever.

The next morning before work, I sat alone in my car, praying. For several months, I had prayed, "God, let Your will be done in my life." That morning, I prayed, "Jesus, if you're real, come into my heart, and let's see what happens." In my wildest imagination, I could not have anticipated what happened next. Immediately, I felt as if burdens I didn't know I had were flung off my shoulders.

God Loves Those Who Hate Him

All my accumulated pain and sorrow fled. In the same instant, I felt as if indescribable love and joy were flooding my being like warm honey.

I knew what I had prayed, I knew now that Jesus was real, but I observed what was happening to me almost in shocked disbelief. I walked to my office in awe, feeling as if I were floating two feet above ground. I could hardly believe that I was now "born-again," yet I understood clearly for the first time why it was called that. It felt as if all the lights in the universe had gone on and I was truly alive for the first time. It was pure, inexpressible, indescribable joy, joy, joy! I was most definitely not the same person I had been before I asked Jesus into my heart. I was ecstatic.

I had finally found The Truth, The Good, The Love, The Beautiful, the God of the universe who reveals himself only through the real person Jesus Christ, not through anyone else. No, not through the Buddha (I had tried meditating), Krishna (I had read about him), Mohammed (I read enough to know he was not the truth), philosophy, psychology, meditation, logic or even religion. "For there is one God and one Mediator between God and men, the Man Christ Jesus" (1 Timothy 2:5).

Later that day, alone in my room, I remembered that the only times I had used Jesus' name was with profanity. I became alarmed and thought, "Oh no! Could he forgive me for that?" No sooner had the question entered my mind than I felt a loving supernatural embrace. It was then, for the first time, that I understood that I was a sinner who did not deserve mercy, and yet, mercifully, in the same fraction of a second, I was forgiven of all my sins. How could it be that the God that I had hated, and whose followers I had

From Myth to Belief

despised, had loved me so much that he stooped to my level to help me to believe in Him!?

The next day, sitting in the kitchen and thinking, in awe of Christ's love, I suddenly thought of my father. A year or so prior, I had forgiven my father, or so I thought. I had come, through popular psychology, to the point where I understood why my father had been the way he had been (I had found out he had also been treated roughly as a child) and I felt sorry for him. But now, I knew what true forgiveness felt like. Having received Christ into my heart, when I thought of my father, I felt rivers of love flowing freely through me toward him. I now understood that one can only truly and completely forgive another when he has been forgiven by God through receiving Jesus personally.

Now, I actually thank God for my childhood pain because it propelled me to seek the truth, to seek the one who is good, loving and kind, but is above human reasoning. If P, (God exists), then Q (He is loving and kind and doesn't want me to suffer). P was true. Q was also true. Though my suffering grieved Him, He did not intervene. But, ultimately, He brought good out of evil, because the pain caused me to search for Him with all my heart (Deuteronomy 4:29) and to seek and find the truth which set me free (John 8:32). I found the truth, not through logic, but according to the loving, merciful and simple terms of Him who reigns supreme above all logic and human reasoning. "...Unless one is born again, he cannot see the kingdom of God" (John 3:3). It was not when I reasoned in my mind, but when I invited Jesus into my life, that I experienced this: "He has delivered us from the power of darkness and conveyed us into the kingdom of

God Loves Those Who Hate Him

the Son of His love, in whom we have redemption through His blood, the forgiveness of sins" (Colossians 1:13-14).

Following my born again experience, I couldn't wait to hear from my Heavenly Father every day. I excitedly opened the Bible to hear His voice. When my earthly father had disciplined me, I felt overwhelmed by his anger. When my Heavenly Father corrected me, which was often, I felt consumed by His love and goodness. My earthly father had told me in anger that I should never have been born. My Heavenly Father told me lovingly, "Before I formed you in the womb I knew you" (Jeremiah 1:5). He told me that He willed me to be born and that He was so glad that I was born (John 1:13). Jesus flooded my soul with peace: "Peace I leave with you, My peace I give to you; not as the world gives do I give to you. Let not your heart be troubled, neither let it be afraid" (John 14:27). And Jesus further assured me that He was preparing a place for me in Heaven (John 14:1-3).

Years later, God led me to my dying father's hospital bed. As my father lay there quietly, I clearly felt God's embrace and prompting at just the right moment to share Christ's love and forgiveness. "The time is now! Now!" I felt God say in my spirit. After my father passed away later that night, God gave me a vision of my father shooting rapidly through space, and then I heard him gasp in awe at the beauty of what he was seeing and hearing. I was not able to see what he saw, but I knew it was incomprehensibly glorious by the sound of his voice. He had lived on this earth admiring manmade beauty. But, having received Christ in his final hours on earth, he entered into God's presence, finding a beauty unrivaled and unimaginable on

From Myth to Belief

this earth.

Years earlier, a voice had told me, "He's very beautiful!" Now, my father also knew that He, the most beautiful of all because of His love and personal sacrifice for us, is Jesus.

I have now been married for fifteen years to that same Christian friend who lovingly and sacrificially introduced me to the real Jesus, the One who is alive and dwells in the hearts of men, women and children who invite Him in. I pray that those who know Jesus will be emboldened, despite persecution, mockery, hatred, slander, cursing, or intimidation, to share the Truth in love with those who so desperately need Him, however they seem to reject Him outwardly, for only God knows the heart of a man.

My husband, George, and I have three boys ages ten, seven and four. We are far from perfect parents, but we cherish our children, knowing they are gifts from God, knowing that God has a plan for their lives. It is only through God's love and grace and our ongoing surrender to Him that we are able to raise them with wisdom, tenderness and patience, disciplining them in love.

We sometimes make mistakes. We sometimes lose our tempers. But, God helps us daily to be more patient and appreciate them as He made them. We have rejoiced to see our oldest, Nico, accept Jesus into his heart with tears, moved by Jesus' love for him. We have been delighted by our second son, Isaac's kindness and forgiveness toward friends who have stolen, lied and treated him unkindly, and by his invitations to them to hear about and receive the love of Christ (several have). We are tickled to hear our four year old Samuel sing, "JESUS, you're my best FRIEND, You will always be, nothing can E-E-E-VER change that!"

God Loves Those Who Hate Him

Jesus. My Jesus, My Lord and Savior. The Truth. The Good. The Beautiful. There's no one like Him. No love like His. He loved me and pursued me with His love and mercy even when I hated Him and those who loved Him. He helped me to believe. All things are possible with God.

Oakland, California
As I heard the story from Shari Argyropoulos

From an Anarchist Atheist to a Useful Christian

Anarchists may become useful to societies when they find meaning in their lives.

With humility and immeasurable gratitude, I realize that what God has allowed to happen in my life was just to bring me closer to him. Looking back, I see and understand the special learning experiences that molded my character in my search for truth in life.

My parents were immigrants. My father was a Greek from Daphne, and my mother was an Italian from Palermo. Strange to say, but neither my father nor my mother really knew God, and neither had any desire to teach me of Him other than in the critical moments of imminent death we faced a few times. My relatives tell me I was given the "last rights" several times: once when I was too little to remember, then again at the age of nine when I suffered from acute appendicitis, and finally when I attempted suicide at twenty-three (my second attempt).

The case of appendicitis was particularly important, because I had no religious education. Feeling death approaching fast, I was desperately seeking to say the right prayer. At the time, I vaguely believed in heaven, and the only thing that my mother had taught me from her Catholic upbringing was that God is One. That one God I had to

From an Anarchist Atheist to a Useful Christian

find on my own, I was told, because only he would allow me to go to his heaven when I died. My problem, however, was that I did not even know his name! As doctors and nurses frantically prepared me for emergency surgery, an uninvited priest walked into my room and stood next to my bed.

"Good evening," he said formally. He immediately added, "I came to pray for you." He made the sign of the cross in front of my surprised face without asking me, and asked me to repeat after him as he recited a prayer. I had never heard this prayer in my life, but of course, I repeated it. It began with "Hail Mary." He recited first, I repeated after him till we finished the prayer. Once finished, he asked me to kiss the "Cross of Christ." This I did too, but inside I was very confused. I addressed a prayer to one person, Mary, and I kissed the cross of another person, of Christ. Didn't mom say that there is only one God? Which one of these two will take me to heaven? Is Mary above Christ or Christ above Mary? I wondered. The feelings of uncertainty and insecurity inside made me sink into disappointment as the nurses pushed my bed quickly to the operating room from which I did not believe I would come out alive. Finally, after the heroic efforts of the doctors, I did come out alive, and so I did not need either Christ or the Virgin Mary.

As the years went by, I regret to say, I was deprived from the things of God. They did not send me to Sunday school, and no one answered my persistent, though rare, questions about why we go to church. Many years later, I realized that my parents did not know why we went to church either. They just wanted to maintain some connection with the religious and ecclesiastical system, because they were

From Myth to Belief

taught in their culture that this was a fundamental principle of their lives and society. While growing up, I began to doubt. I began to search for reasons.

At fifteen, I arrived at certain conclusions. Nobody was sure about the system. Yet no one dared challenge it, because what would people say? All would despise them, even the ones who denied or implicitly questioned the system. Still, I thought, who cares what the people think? Whom are we kidding? Nobody really knew God for sure. Yet we all pretended. I compared the case with The Emperor's New Clothes. At sixteen, I therefore became an atheist. How I found the courage to announce it to my mother, I do not know. She was saddened, but there was no fight. She was speechless. And what could she say?

I started down the road of searching for the truth, which was very long and very rough. It led first to philosophy, then psychology, medical science, sociology. I discovered that many of these studies deadened my conscience. So I ended up a rebel at home and with family; an anarchist against society, authority and the status quo, because I did not want to put up with playing games anymore. I could not bear to be phony. At that point, I could not understand that it was easier for God to work in the heart of an anarchist rather than in the cruel heart of a lukewarm Christian hypocrite. The curious thing was that at that dark period of my life, no one talked to me about God. Even if someone talked to me, I may have not liked to listen. But God used something amazing to catch my attention.

I was nineteen, and lolling on a sofa in a gathering of bohemian artists (which was then a colorful term for those who refused to find a regular job). The debate suddenly took

From an Anarchist Atheist to a Useful Christian

an interesting turn. A young girl started to say something about the Bible. I had no idea what the Bible was, and I felt even more ignorant after this girl claimed the Bible was a wonderful poetry book. I knew the girl, of course, that she lived it up and did whatever pleased her. And right there, a young man made the following statement,

"If I were to get religion and go to church, I would become a Jew." That statement made me sit up amazed and ask,

"How could this be? You're an Irish-American. You're not a Jew!"

"Oh, it does not matter," he said with a dose of disapproval.

"Yes, but why would you want to follow the Jewish religion?"

"Because," replied he, "Jews are the only ones who follow the Bible." (Of course, now I know that this is not exactly so, but he said what he thought he knew.)

"And what has the Bible to do with the Church?" I continued asking in my ignorance.

"Don't you know that all the churches say they are based on the Bible, but only the Jews apply what the Bible says?" he replied. It hit me like a rock. Now I knew where churches came from. Now I knew who started that system, that tradition. I lolled back on the couch, but I remember contemplating this thought: if I ever decide to go to church, or at least understand it, I must first read the Bible.

More years went by, more sin entered my life. Now, I've got to say with all sense of truth that I was not aware of what I was doing, and I'm not saying this to justify myself. Of course, I did not want to be arrested, but I had

From Myth to Belief

no hesitation or regret of what I was doing. The reasoning was as follows. The system is rotten, and they're all crooks anyway. What's the difference between tax-evasion and me hitting up a few stores? What benefits do they get by going to church or by believing in God? Let Him protect them once they get caught. I was tired of church-goers and all the sinners who wore a large cross and robbed the world, while I simply committed petty thefts. The only difference between what they did and what I did was that their robberies were socially acceptable. Ok, so they did not respect other citizens or their Christian followers. But didn't they even respect the Godthey preached about? Maybe they did not even believe in God. But, if there was a God somewhere out there, what did they think of Him? That he was deaf? Or blind? Or plain dumb? I laughed to myself and ridiculed them, "What theater they play!" And I hit them as hard as I could.

More years passed. I had two nervous breakdowns, I visited a psychiatrist several times, and later, I even did group psychotherapy. I was in and out of hospitals, clinics and other institutions. It was then that I added psychiatry to my ways of seeking truth. I was looking for love and happiness everywhere, and I could not find them.

This disappointed me so much that I made my second attempt at suicide. But then, I realized that there must be a God, because there is no way that anyone survives after taking the huge amount of drugs that I had ingested, unless something people call "a miracle" had happened to me. I was awed by Someone or Something bigger than me that allowed me to live. I remember wondering if it was what people called God. Or was it some Higher Power?

From an Anarchist Atheist to a Useful Christian

And because I did not know, I "promoted" myself from a fanatical atheist to a passive agnostic. I longed to ask someone, but I hesitated, because I was afraid they would once again spit out the same old disgusting stories, telling me that I should spend my whole life bowing down and kissing icons or statues, carrying some talisman, repeating a particular prayer, or making the sign of the cross, perhaps even suggesting I go to a witch. I knew and understood that all these were meaningless ceremonial stuff.

I remember that during this time, I was approached by the Jehovah's Witnesses. They assured me they were studying the Bible and that caught my attention. I even went to their "church" a couple of times. It seemed to me that something was not right with them, but I did not know what. After coming out of their "church meetings" I did not have peace in my heart. It felt like I had not met God there. I was afraid and quit immediately.

It was then that my best friend talked to me about her aunt in Europe. She said she knew her well and that she was a genuine Christian, because she drew strength from God through faith in him, and it allowed her to face all the tragedies she suffered for years. I had not heard anything like this before. I remember that I cried to myself,

"This is the God I am looking for! Do not talk to me about a sunny-Sunday-in-church-when-all-is-rosy-God. I am trying to find the God who will keep me steady in times of earthquake."

I finally found Him, the One and Only God, in a small country church in June 1966. His name is Jesus. When I read and understood the Bible, the Gospel, I concluded that He is the Only and Truly Holy God of Heaven and

From Myth to Belief

Earth and that I should never pity him. Then I felt the Holy Spirit inviting me: "Christ wants you to come into his arms." And I said,

"Oh my God, I want it so much, but I'm not sure how I can live a life that pleases you. I've got to leave my rebellion, my anarchy, my sin behind." He asked me,

"Did you find happiness in all your activities, in all the places you looked?"

"No," I answered without hesitating.

"Then learn that only I offer the love you're looking for everywhere," he assured. And it was like he anointed my head with myrrh.

It is impossible to describe precisely the supernatural love of God that I felt then, but there is no doubt in me about it. At that very moment, I dedicated my whole self to God forever. "Therefore I was buried with Him through baptism into death" (Romans 6:4). "I died, and my life is hidden with Christ in God" (Colossians 3:3). Now "I am sealed with the Holy Spirit" (2 Corinthians 1:22). But something else happened simultaneously.

Almost immediately, I realized that there are multitudes of people, just like me, who are not aware of how much God loves them! And immediately I also felt the need to tell them that Christ is alive, that he loves them and he wants them close to him! When you meet the living God, you cannot but want to share the news. So, one should be an active, rather than a passive, Christian.

Well, a former anarchist, me, a former atheist, me, I became an activist in the Christian Association of Suffolk City College. I started out as a member, and later I successfully became Secretary, Vice President and

From an Anarchist Atheist to a Useful Christian

President. The main task of the Association is to have open, public debates to discuss the religions of the world, all religions, twice a week.

At the same time, I made sure to get my degree in theology. So I taught at the Institute of Biblical Education of Long Island in New York and other religious institutions. I also did seminars of interest to women and authored a number of religious articles that have appeared in religious publications.

Another activity that I love is my continued collaboration with Greeks for Christ International through which, among many other things, I have served in a medical clinic on a Greek island in the Aegean Sea as a medical and hospital assistant.

By the grace of God, he has allowed me to work in his "vineyard." From the day I walked into his kingdom, I have had the opportunity to speak about Christ to many people. I know that God is with me, regardless of problems I may face. And this is the significant difference and the secret of a dynamic Christian life: "It is no longer I who live, but Christ lives in me" (Galatians 2:20). All these years I have seen many turn to Christ as I did. But others I've seen turn to Christ in a calculating way, with the wrong motives.

Many people approach him only when they have problems to solve, some offering him offerings in exchange of his favor, and others turn to him just to be cured from illnesses. It is true that we all need God's help, but it is of key importance to have our hearts filled with gratitude for his love that can save us from sin (2 Peter 3:9). Everything else will follow. "God rewards those who sincerely seek Him and seek not what he can give them" (Hebrews 11:6).

From Myth to Belief

That's why "we are saved from sin by virtue of his grace" (Ephesians 2:8,9). Personally, I believe if God had done nothing for me but save me, giving me a "new nature" (John 1:12) and revealing his face to me again and again, it would be enough. I deserve none of this. Like David in Psalms 8:4, I say "What is man that You are mindful of him, and the son of man that You visit him?" Because God did not create life and then abandon us. We have only ourselves to blame if we deny him, "for God so loved the world that He gave His only begotten Son, that whoever believes in Him should not perish but have everlasting life" (John 3:16).

Who would have thought that an atheist like me would someday turn around and hug the King of Kings and the Lord of Lords? Who would imagine that an anarchist like me would be useful to society? Only by the mercy of God can this be true. That's why I thank God the Father, Son and Holy Spirit, now and always!

Mastic, New York
As I heard the story from Dorothy Stassinopoulos

I Don't Want to Die!

It's the law of life:
You must die before you start living.

George limped slightly from birth. He was short, thin and sickly. Nonetheless, George was always well-dressed and polite-mannered. His mind cut like a Quattro razor blade.

George was a successful businessman. When planning his business, his keen mind's eye could foresee even the tiniest future details, so he knew the outcome in advance. He had common sense, the common characteristic of successful entrepreneurs and so uncommon amongst failed ones. So George built a small estate of houses, farms and cars in his hometown of Provo, Utah. He drove the most expensive car in town; a unique yellow and beautiful Marmon cabrio.

Even at the age of twenty-eight, he was so successful and well-known that people repeatedly asked him to run for mayor. He always replied, smiling, "Pass this honor to a respected politician, please. I'm just a businessman."

George was born and raised in the quiet village of Theoktisto, Arcadia in southern Greece in the late 19th century. That's also where he finished high school, which meant he was an educated Greek for his time. However, at eighteen years old, he left the village in a hurry. Rather, his father kicked him out because George had almost

From Myth to Belief

killed a young man who had "harassed" his sister. After leaving Greece, George ended up in Utah.

Winters in Utah are bitter, cold, filled with snow and frost. George being sickly by nature passed his winters ill, most often severely. Many times his sufferings came to a head, and he visited the brink of death. Being loaded with money, however, he enjoyed the best hospital care money could buy. He constantly surrounded himself with beautiful women who would care for him. Somehow, he would always manage to live for another year. In the deep of winter, George would secretly wish he would die so his miserable life would end.

When the winter was over, George came out like a badger from his hole and lived his life fully. He never missed a premiere at a theater, opera or classical music event. He would attend dances, always accompanied by at least two beautiful women. Even in clubs or bars, everyone knew him and treated him with a drink. When he left the place, he'd buy drinks for the whole house before bidding farewell to all. Everyone liked and respected him.

His personal physician advised him day and night that if he wanted to live, he needed to give up everything in Provo and go live in Arizona where the climate is hot and dry. The physician kept ringing a bell of warning that things could not go on like this forever. "Someday, you are going to get really sick and kick the bucket," the doctor kept saying.

George wouldn't listen. What would he be without his business, his properties and his friends? Sometimes we are held prisoner by the life we lead, by our business or by our family and friends. We won't move an inch even if we

I Don't Want to Die!

know it is for our own good. George knew this; he would nod half-hearted agreement to his doctor, telling him that he would get around to moving someday. Instead, many times he contemplated driving his Marmon fast into a tree so that all his sufferings will be over once and for all.

The doctor's prediction was fulfilled when George was thirty-two. During a freezing cold winter, George got deathly sick. He was diagnosed with phthisis. He had double pneumonia, and his lungs had filled with fluid, causing cardiac complications. His personal physician was by his side twenty-four hours a day. All his friends had gathered at the hospital. They had even arranged for the funeral as everyone waited for George's last breath.

"Poor man..."

"He's leaving us so young..."

"He should have listened to his doctor..." the friends whispered among themselves.

The dying man was already in another world, that of a coma. With the help of an oxygen machine, he breathed heavily, aslow rattle of death. But he continued breathing. Half the winterpasted. Slowly, as George stayed in a coma, his friends left oneby one. After all, they had jobs, families and personal lives. Onlythe most devoted of his girlfriends stayed behind. Eventuallythough, even they left him. Finally, only the nurses remained.

One particular morning, George opened his eyes. He was alone in a place he knew all too well: a hospital room. It felt like a second home. He removed the oxygen mask and the IV line. He got up and went to the bathroom adjacent to his room to wash and shave. He returned to his room, dressed, sat on the edge of the bed and called

From Myth to Belief

the nurse. She ran to him and got the shock of her life.

"I'm hungry," he said. Then he added, "And call me a taxi."

Immediately, the nurse ran straight to the doctors. She also called George's personal doctor.

The doctors tried to persuade him to stay in the hospital to recover completely. They emphasized that he had only six months to live. If he went out in the freezing cold in his condition, it'd be plain suicide. He'd be dead within a week, maybe as soon as he crossed through the hospital door.

But George would not listen. He had made up his mind. He had heard there was a narrow highway in California, running the length of her coast: Highway 1. It starts at the border with Mexico and crawls like a snake on the coastal mountaintops, continues through the states of Oregon and Washington and ends up in Canada. It's a uniquely beautiful and deadly dangerous drive. At times, you drive next to the ocean, a constant companion whose waves lap softly against the beach like a whispering seductress at your feet, as it happens in the southern part of the state in Santa Barbara. Then, you drive on incredibly tight bends next to a loud and angry white ocean trying to swallow you a thousand or more feet below your feet, as it happens in the north-middle part of the state from San Francisco to San Luis Obispo.

It was there George had decided to go end his miserable life.

Within a few days, he had made arrangements for his business. He said he would be away on vacation for a few weeks. His friends were happy that George was

I Don't Want to Die!

finally serious about his health. George got in his Marmon and drove west on Freeway 80, the one that cuts the U.S. horizontally from New York to San Francisco. He drove the 850 miles nonstop, like a horse with blinders on, single-minded to reach Highway 1 located on the end of America and the end of his life.

Late in the afternoon the next day, he arrived in ever-sunny San Francisco. He went straight to the "Greek Town" in the city center, located at 3rd and Folsom Street on the south side of Market Street. He planned to grab some Greek food to eat as his last supper, then he'd take a walk in the Greek town, and later he'd go sleep in a neighborhood hotel. The next morning he'd get up early to take Highway 1 to Los Angeles. He would find the highest point, perhaps the Devil's Slide, to go down the cliff and end it all. He had arranged everything in his mind... up to the most infinitesimal detail.

He walked in a grocery store owned by a Greek. However, the shopkeeper was closing. As George was talking with the man, he told him that he too was Greek, he was traveling and had just come from Utah. The shopkeeper invited him home for dinner. George saw that the grocer was spoiling his own plans, but the grocer was being politely stubborn like a true, hospitable Greek. George had to give in.

When they arrived at the grocer's home, the host ordered his wife to add another set on the table and his little children to make their room available overnight for the guest. At dinner, George shared briefly about his business in Provo. He said he was on vacation in California, but he was careful to avoid any mention of his plans.

From Myth to Belief

When dinner was over, George got up, eyes half-closed from fatigue and good food, and started to his room to sleep even though it was only about 7 o'clock.

"Oh, no, dear friend. First we go to church," said the host in a way that left no room for discussion.

"To church!?" asked George, eyes wide open in surprise. "What's today? Christmas or Resurrection service?" He asked incredulously.

"Maybe it's resurrection, for you..." said the host between being serious and funny.

When they entered the church, the service had already begun. The preacher at the pulpit was preaching.

George wondered, "What business do I have here? I got other plans."

He cursed the minute he entered the grocery store. They sat somewhere in the back pews. He looked around. Some people were dressed simply and others formally. It was a typical congregation. The preacher continued to talk about things George did not understand. But in a particular moment, the speaker suddenly stopped and proposed the question: "Where will you go if you die right now?"

Suddenly this question became like a heavy hammer that struck George right between the eyes. He had planned his death in every detail, but he failed to provide answers to this question. He had not even thought about it. The preacher continued his preaching for another hour yet. George heard nothing else. The only question he could ask himself was: "After I die tomorrow, where am I going?"

There was a great struggle inside him. He was so discouraged by his life that he wanted to die. But he also

I Don't Want to Die!

felt like a fool for planning to end his life without foreseeing where he would end up. He, who was successful because he had common sense! How could he be so blind this time around? It was as if someone had tricked him.

So great was the struggle within him, so heavy was the conviction inside him, so huge was the uncertainty he found himself in that he jumped up from his seat and ran to the preacher shouting: "I DON'T WANT TO DIE! I DON'T WANT TO DIE!"

There he fell before the altar and cried like a baby. Who? George, the most reputable businessman, the most cosmopolitan, the most prominent citizen of the city of Provo, Utah. The preacher stopped his preaching, stepped down from the pulpit, hugged George and wept along with him. When they got up after a while, George had left at the altar his old, sick life. He was another, brand new, happy man.

When George left Provo, the doctors told him that he had at most six months to live, but maybe as little as a week. George, believe it or not, lived for another fifty-five years! The best part? He never got sick again. Not even a runny nose.

George traveled throughout America several times telling his story to whoever listened. He became a preacher himself! He preached: "Many times we try to decide how to dispose of our life without taking God into account, but we do not own our lives. The most important thing is that God really cares for us, and if we allow Him, He can perform wonders in our life, even if our life is not worth anything in our own eyes."

One glorious morning after many full days, George left

this earth with a final smile etched on his lips. He knew where he was going.

Provo, Utah; San Francisco, California
As I heard the story from Rev. George J. Samartzis

What Should I Do to Become a Good Christian?

> *"One sows and another reaps. I sent you to reap that for which you have not labored. Others have labored."*
>
> John 4:37-38

Costas was a typical Greek Christian. He attended church, well, not every Sunday, but at least on Christmas and Easter. He did the sign of the cross and lit a candle, but he did not participate in the liturgy, because such a thing was forbidden at his church. But he took communion regularly. He also frequently confessed to the priest and invited him home for agiasmos or blessing of the house. And always he kissed the priest's hand.

He was proud of his Christian religion, even though he had never read the Bible or the Fathers, just as he was proud of his Greekness even though he had never read Homer's Odyssey or any of the classic Greek authors, ancient or contemporary. For him, whoever was not like him was an enemy of Christ and of the Fatherland, and he was not Greek (as if Jesus was Greek!).

He lived in San Francisco, and like the rest of the United States since its birth in 1776, there was religious tolerance. Anyone had the right to stand up and say whatever they wanted for whatever god they believe in, and they were

From Myth to Belief

protected by the law.

In the early 20th century, many Greeks migrated to America for a better future. Many of them heard new things, unknown in the Fatherland. The world opened for those people. They encountered and accepted fresh ideas. They found new ways of life. They saw new, unexplored horizons. The most adventurous of them, like the truly Greek Odysseus, rushed to know them, conquer them, embrace them.

Of these people, some heard of a personal, living relationship with God through Jesus Christ, something completely new and revolutionary for people who previously stood solemnly in church occupying a standing-pew in silence, hearing the gospel sung to them in an ancient language they did not understand and remaining foreign to what was happening around them. They heard that Jesus was not just for the world 2,000 years ago, but that he is alive for today's people, for today's Greeks. They heard that Jesus did not heal only in ancient times, but he heals now, even though he is not present in flesh and bone. Also, they heard that he saves people from their sins now as then, that he gives peace to the hearts of people even now, and that he actually helps them to be successful and happy in their daily lives today, now.

In other words, they saw their own religion, which they knew for years, the one they had learned from generation to generation, the one they always knew that was a living question, now coming alive, in action, and in practical application. They embraced it. And they began in good faith to share with other fellow Greeks the treasure they had found.

What Should I Do to Become a Good Christian?

On Sunday afternoons when they did not work, young Greeks visited Greek coffee shops and diners in Greek town in San Francisco at 3rd and Folsom, and later at Eddy and Market streets. They talked to their compatriots about what they had found, gave them New Testaments (in today's Greek language of course), and sometimes they prayed with them, if the compatriots asked for prayer. Among them was someone by the name of Nathan, a hardworking, easy going, faithful Christian.

Once Nathan and the rest left, Costas would show up and snatch the New Testaments away from the hands of the compatriots. He tore and destroyed them in front of their surprised eyes and left swearing. Sometimes he'd even wait for them so he could drive them away, adorning them brutally with many "decorative" adjectives. Sometimes he would follow them, mocking and making gestures to signify that they were paid to share the gospel, or that they were crazy. In short, he made their life quite difficult. Indeed, rumors circulated that he consulted with the officials of his church to interfere in any way possible.

Costas had become a big problem for those Greeks of Northern California in the 1930s, '40s and '50s. They did not know how to deal with him. By talking to him? By protesting? With a lawsuit? How? And, because they did not know what to do, they started praying for him regularly. Then, in order to avoid him, they visited a different coffee shop in a different neighborhood every time, so they always talked to different people. But, somehow, he always found them. And Costas did not change.

Many, many years went by. All these young people got old and died, including Nathan. But there were more

From Myth to Belief

new Greeks than there were old ones. So many, in fact, that now they were not only in Northern California, but had spread to many other cities, states and even other countries. They had also started to operate a school, to publish tracts and magazines, to produce and broadcast radio shows and television programs so that the Word of God was heard everywhere through all media, print, broadcast and later on the internet.

Sometime in 1980s, the new, young speaker of the Greek radio show *The Greek Hour of Hope* received a letter from a listener in San Francisco, who heard the program on the station covering Northern California. The listener wrote,

"I was born a brat, I grew up a skunk and I aged into a dirty old man. I've done everything my Church orders. I confess, take communion, make the sign of the cross, bow down prostrate; but I have not yet found peace in my heart. Tell me, please, what should I do to become a good Christian? And I will do it if I can."

The speaker sent him a note that he would respond on the next show which was dedicated to him, and asked him not to miss it. Indeed, in the next radio broadcast, the speaker spoke personally to him, in a manner of speaking, through the radio.

"There is no need for you to perform certain religious duties. There is no need for you to do anything to become a child of God because Jesus did everything for you on the cross when he died in your place, when he took your sins and your guilt off of your shoulders in order to liberate you and give you peace. Just accept His work for you in faith, and you are saved."

What Should I Do to Become a Good Christian?

In a few days, the speaker received a second letter from the same listener who wrote, among other things, "I believed exactly as you told me on the radio and now I can sleep at night. I have peace in my heart, because I took care of my eternal future. I thank Christ who died for me, a sinner. I thank God who loved and accepted even me. And I thank you, who told me to do so. And if you were here, I would embrace and kiss you, my brother speaker, with all my heart."

Nathan's wife, Sofia, now old but spry, with a razor-sharp mind and an elephant's memory, was listening to *The Greek Hour of Hope* radio program. As a matter of fact, she listened regularly and supported it financially. She, then, asked the speaker,

"What's the name of that man in San Francisco, son, whom you spoke about on the radio?"

"Costas...," he responded.

As soon as she heard the full name, Yaya (grandma) Sofia's eyes turned skyward. She raised her hands and cried out to God, "Great are you Lord, and marvelous are your works!" And then, turning to the speaker she said, "Now, sit right here and listen to Costas's story," and she went on to tell it in detail.

In two years, Costas died at the age of ninety-two. No doubt, those young people whom he had once insulted, persecuted and driven away were surprised to see him walking through the glorious gate of heaven. And they praised God for their prayers, prayers that were certainly not wasted.

San Francisco, California

Changes in Prisoner's Lives

I was called to prison ministry while recuperating from a tragic auto accident that had brought me to the Lord. I heard an audible voice call me in the middle of the day as I was reading the Word of God. The voice of the Lord said in a powerful but gentle way, "The prisoners need you!"

I then saw a vision of men behind prison bars and felt so bad to see human beings living in cages. My spirit felt their hopelessness and despair. I strongly felt they needed to know about Jesus like I did, for them to know He is real and to know Him in a personal way, that He loves them and died for their sins as He did for all. I looked down and found my finger on the verse Matthew 25:36, "When I was in prison, you visited me." The voice, the vision, and then the Word, all in a moment. I cried and travailed for these lost souls. At the time I didn't understand why God showed me this and gave me this burden.

I've been faithfully going into men's prisons weekly for over twenty years, preaching and teaching the Word of God. My life's story (or testimony) is a powerful and effective tool for these inmates — showing a changed life because changed lives change lives! The Lord showed me Luke 4:18, "The Spirit of the Lord is upon me. He has anointed me to preach...deliverance to the captives."

It's a blessing to be called to one of the greatest harvest fields there is. It is very ripe for picking. Revival is now coming behind prison walls. They're finding out there is no other answer but JESUS! Every human being has a hunger in his heart that they try to feed with something or other. A lot of inmates grew up with some church background but have fallen away like a prodigal son, but God is ABLE to turn things around when they return, totally surrender their lives, and come back home. Isaiah 55:11 says the Word of God never returns void. It accomplishes what it is sent to do. The Lord is waiting for His chosen with open arms and we are to be JESUS for the unsaved world. We are all sinners saved by His Amazing Grace. He's a God of second chances.

When convicts see a real person who had a changed life and is a walking miracle, it makes them understand what God can do in their lives. It brings them HOPE. It becomes an open door for them to receive Him. Many have told me when they accept Jesus into their lives that they are happier and feel more free in prison than they ever did on the outside. It's the Prince of Peace now ruling in their hearts. The Holy Spirit takes over and becomes their real teacher, their healer of past wounds and comforter, the one who convicts them of sin, and guides them in all their ways. As they grow in him, they too will pass on that Light. Luke 7:47 says, "Those who have been forgiven much, love much."

For more than twenty years, I've seen many souls come to the saving knowledge of Jesus Christ through my own life's story and especially the Word of God. It's a key to open the heart's door of the incarcerated. I have gang members and repeat offenders come into my class and ask me, how do I change? How do I get rid of this anger inside my heart? I tell them the answer is a man named Jesus. Give Him a chance and repent (turn around). Then in walks JESUS, who changes the inner spirit to become the new creature in Christ (2 Cor. 5:17). I'm only the messenger and a spiritual mother who picks up the broken vessels in the potter's field. The Potter reforms the clay pots and makes them new for His use. I'm so blessed to see them change and grow in the power of God when they see God's true Agape Love. I've been told by many hardened criminals that God has given me the Key to unlock their hard hearts. It's Jesus' anointing in me that sets the captive free. The anointing breaks the yokes of bondage and the generational curse on their lives.

The fields are white with harvest. Let's go where Jesus sends us. Answer the call and be doers of His Word to bring the lost in. We will be surprised, as Christ says, who we will see in Heaven! John 8:36, "If the Son therefore shall make you free, you shall be free indeed."

**Sera Tsioukas
Easton, Pennsylvania**

Sera Tsioukas lives in Easton, PA with her husband, Gus, and their three daughters, Angela, Alexa and Andrea. They also have a home in the Tarpon Springs, Florida, area where they have lived and still share the gospel when they can.

Sera works as a home health agency nurse to keep her hours flexible to serve the Lord where needed. Gus has worked throughout his life as a computerized numerical controlled machinist. Sera has been in men's prison ministry faithfully for over twenty years in Pennsylvania and Florida. She also speaks wherever the Lord opens doors for her to evangelize the Good News of Jesus Christ. Her husband, Gus, also comes when he is able as they share their life changing testimony, their prophetic visions, and the miracles of God.

They've held home meetings for speakers (including Peter Vourliotis) from around the world to preach in their home for the Lord for more than twenty-five years. Sera also has recently written a movie script of her true life story called "Wild Ride to Heaven," waiting to be produced for the glory of God.

Dangerous Dan

*He looked down, bent his knee and
got a handful of dirt, me. He showed mercy, shed tears.
The dirt became clay and with his affectionate hands,
he made me human.*

The cockroach races would begin soon. The three roaches with assorted colored backs, each with threads tied to their bodies dragging a miniature styro-foam cart, were ready at the starting point at the edge of my blanket. Also ready were the two other players holding a broom straw in their hands in order to prod their cockroach. And gathered around us, all the prisoners were fighting among themselves by encouraging the cockroach they had bet on. Ahhh... How I loved these cockroach races!

As a matter of fact, all three were my cockroaches. They were indeed the way by which I earned my bread. They won me my cigarettes, because cigarettes are the currency of prison. So, I kept them in a beautiful box in my cell and treated them like my pets. I would talk to them, I would caress them, and every day, I would feed them crumbs from my own plate with my own hands. The crumbs I gave to two of the cockroaches, I first soaked in watered-down thyroxin, a drug that made them slow. To mine I gave crumbs dipped in water only, without thyroxin. Thus I always or almost always, won all races, because mine was always faster. Of course, sometimes

Dangerous Dan

I let another cockroach win to not draw any suspicions. I also sold *pruno*, a cheap wine I made to my colleagues for five packs of cigarettes a bottle. These things made me great and "reputable" in prison. Prisons, I should say. Because it took me twenty-two years of life to "graduate" from almost all the prisons of California; CMC East, Chino, Vacaville, Folsom, Soledad and San Quentin.

I never knew my mother, and I hated my father to death. I grew up in the streets of Castro Valley and Oakland, California, and ever since I was a baby, I learned to defend myself to survive. In fact, I did everything I could to survive. At the age of thirteen, I started taking heroin, and immediately followed the drinking, thefts, armed robberies etc. I was in and out of juvenile prison, and later, ordinary prisons. I would get out just long enough for them to arrest me again. I hated everyone and everything around me. Whatever evil one could think of or imagine, I did, whether inside or outside the prison even unheard of crimes. At every opportunity, I'd stab anyone without cause just to see blood running. That was a delightful sight to me! I was so depraved! I was once imprisoned for eleven years. Straight after that, I was thrown even deeper into the system. I spent three year straight naked inside "The Hole," a six feet by six feet by six feet cold, windowless cell made of stainless steel.

My nickname was "Dangerous Dan," because I was the fear and terror of prisons and city streets. I was the coldest, meanest, cruelest; the most bloodthirsty, most powerful, the most dangerous villain in California. Everyone respected me out of fear. And in my dark cell, in the endless hours of night and day, I hated myself for

From Myth to Belief

what I was. I fantasized that I was a normal person with a family. I imagined myself being a father tenderly stroking the hand of an infant, my imaginary son, who certainly did not take after me.

I was thirty-nine years old and just recently out of terrible Folsom prison when I received a telephone call from my brother Martin.

"Danny, you've got to go help our sister. Well, today, that is, right now — she is to be exorcised."

"To be, what?"

"You know, she's a devil worshipper. She attends one of those churches, you know, one of the patriarch's of the Church of Satan who sits in San Francisco."

"No, I have no idea ..."

"Anyway, they just told her it's her turn — to be sacrificed."

"What? Be sacrificed? These old f...."

"Well, she ran away and went hiding to some people who are going to rescue and exorcise her. You've got to go find her now and be with her because you are the strong one. You see, I've got something important to do...," he said, and hastily hung up the phone.

"I'll show them..." I mumbled, and swearing, I got my jacket and went to the address I was given by Martin.

As soon as I entered the house I saw religious icons hanging on the walls, candles of all sizes, statues and other religious objects sitting on the tables and house furniture. "Oh, say, what are all these things? These are all those things they tried to stuff my soul with since I was a kid. I hate all this," I reflected. Indeed. I hated with all my heart whatever had to do with churches, with God,

Dangerous Dan

with Christians. Christians, in fact, I hated even more. When I saw a fellow prisoner going to a prayer meeting or Bible study holding his Bible in hand, I kicked him, spat in his face, swore at him and called him a jerk because I considered him weak. The closest I had come to the Bible was cutting its pages to make cigarettes or to use them as toilet paper when I ran out. I decided, therefore, that I did not belong there, and I turned around to leave.

I didn't have time to make it to the door, however, because they put my half-sister in the middle of the room, wrapped a purple cloak around her and began to beat her with rosaries while mumbling incomprehensible spells. In just a short time, the murmurs gradually rose. They became shrieks resulting in such a fuss that the door opened suddenly, and in walked the police.

We got out the next day. They took my sister to another home, with people who seemed to be different kinds of Christians than the ones from the previous night. As soon as I walked in that house, I noticed some expensive items. I thought that it would be worth the trouble for me to visit this house in the near future, alone. Immediately they began to pray for my sister quietly and coherently. I saw her leaning and lying on the carpeted floor.

Suddenly, as she was on her back, (she is only 4-feet 8-inches and very petite) I listened with astonishment as she spoke in a bass male voice saying:

"YOU ARE NOT ABLE TO HARM ME. YOU CAN'T DO ANYTHING TO ME! DON'T YOU UNDERSTAND WHO I AM? HA HA HA!"

At the same time her body began to rise horizontally and hover about two feet above the floor. I was scared

From Myth to Belief

to death. Immediately, we all grabbed and tried to push her back on the floor, but despite all our efforts we were unable to succeed. And the heavy voice that came out of my sister continued to mock us, swearing at us the exact same curses I swore. As we tried to hold her down the guy next to me shouted, "Jesus." Immediately the body of my sister started to descend, but again it rose and hovered again. The heavy voice continued cursing, but when someone uttered the name of Jesus, the body of my sister came down a little bit. She continued to hover, the voice swearing and mocking us, until suddenly, the door was opened (this time by itself), and a strong wind blew into the room. That wind alone brought the body of my sister back on the floor and stopped the blasphemous voice. At that moment, I didn't know what kind of wind it was. I got goose bumps when I realized the two conflicting forces of divinity and evil battling against each other in front of my very eyes.

I had always believed that there was no such thing as god or devil. But here I had both the devil and God in front of me. I had a clear proof that Jesus was stronger than Satan, since only after hearing the name of Jesus, the devil immediately fell back. As for me, I had served the loser, the weaker opponent for many years. I conducted myself, swore and talked just like him; the devil that I had just seen and heard. Who had fooled me? Who had cheated me, me, the strong one; so that I served not the strong, but a weak leader?

With these thoughts I reached the entrance of the house and stood in front of a huge picture of Jesus that adorned the entrance. At that moment, I remembered what I had

Dangerous Dan

always said, that "if God exists, let him prove himself to me and I will believe in him." I stopped and began talking to the picture while looking at him in the eye.

"So, you are true, that is, you're alive, and I thought you did not even exist..."

Having experienced all this with my sister was enough. I had proof. There was no longer any doubt whatsoever for me that God exists and so does the devil.

The hostess of the house and her husband had followed me and stood beside me without me having noticed them. As they were looking along with me at the picture the woman said, "I would have liked for her brother to be here, that one who's always in jail, that sick, cruel, mean and wicked man."

"I'm he," I replied sheepishly.

She was shocked, but she knelt right there in front of me lifting her hands and thanking God.

"Do you want to invite Jesus into your heart?" her husband asked me.

"I do not understand what you say, but I think I need to do something, even now," I replied.

"If you want your life changed, repeat this prayer after me, but do it with your heart, not with your mind. I will not pray for you. I will only help you to pray. That wind that blew in the room and calmed your sister down was the Holy Spirit and he can change you too." When I finished praying, I felt like a huge sack of bricks I carried throughout my whole life had fallen off my back. Suddenly I felt free. I felt like a different person.

Meanwhile, the others continued to pray for my sister but without real effect. Then my girlfriend Berta, who had

From Myth to Belief

grown up in a good church in Hawaii, recalled how any man of God who was full of the Holy Spirit could pray for my sister to be free from demons. She opened the Yellow Pages, turned to "Churches" and began calling them on the phone one by one. She explained the purpose of the call and asked for help. The priest of the first church had to prepare for the Sunday service. The next one was taking his wife shopping. The third was running to catch a plane. She skipped the Greek church, thinking that they may not speak English. The next priest had to attend a clergy dinner and everyone else had some important work to do. Soon Berta ran out of churches, and she had to go back and call the only church she had skipped.

The Greek pastor said that he would gladly come, but he needed three days to fast and pray before he did. In three days the pastor came. He prayed for my sister and thirteen demons came out of her. The last and most difficult one was the demon of suicide.

Immediately I began worshipping at the Greek Church. The pastor sent me to a detox institution and Bible school. My time there was not easy. I suddenly found life very different from that which I was used to, although the program was almost as severe as that of the prison. The devil did not want to lose me, so he attacked me violently. I took off from the school and went back to my old ways, drinking and getting high. In the middle of the night I called the pastor, woke him up, and tried to strike a conversation with him, not because he was my pastor, but because I considered him my friend. He understood. He came out to the streets at two, three, or four o'clock in the morning to find me in a phone booth where I waited for him. He

Dangerous Dan

literally loaded me in his station wagon and returned me to school.

Eventually, I stopped taking off. I complied with the regulations of the school and studied the rest of the time without interruption. In one full year, I, who knew neither to read nor to write when I started that school, graduated! One Sunday morning, I presented my "degree" to the congregation of the Greek Church, and said,

"This is the first and only important thing I've done so far in my life, and I'm proud of it. Thank you to all of you that have encouraged and stood behind me." I had learned to read and write by studying the Bible. Now, I love the Bible and I study it with passion every day.

Immediately after that, I finished another program at a technical school and started working as a welder. The money I was making was disappointing compared to the bunches of hundred-dollar bills from selling drugs that lined my pockets in the old times. But for the first time in my life, I was happy, because I was making an honest wage.

And as soon as I found a job, I married Berta. Our pastor conducted a real Hawaiian wedding in a Greek Church! He even helped us to adopt a son! Together with my wife, I enrolled in a Bible school. We completed the required courses and classes together and we graduated together. So I was ordained a lay-pastor! Who? Me. "Dangerous Dan," who just a little while ago hated everyone including myself. God, however, showed me in a wonderful way that He cares and loves even me and my family. And my sister, who has accepted Christ and changed her life, was baptized in the Holy Spirit, and she now attends church in her hometown. And my father, whom I now love very

From Myth to Belief

much, has accepted Christ into his life. What a wonderful work of change, what a miraculous salvation to an entire family! And the blessings of God have not stopped yet.

Four years after all this took place, God gave me a vision and a mission to search and find homeless people in my hometown. Along with my wife and the youth of the Greek Church, I began a special ministry to those scattered souls of our affluent society which we called *Pro-ject Love*. We make appointments with local supermarkets and, after we introduce our mission, we ask them to give us (free of charge) any food overstock available, and they do. Every second Saturday of the month, we all stuff hundreds of brown bags with lunch in the Dining Hall of the Greek Church. Then, armed with this food, we walk in groups of two on the streets of our downtown, where homeless people usually are.

We search and locate these unhappy people, wrapped in their sad rags, who push all their household belongings in a supermarket cart and sleep on two meters borrowed land for that night only. These people were once doctors, lawyers, or big company executives as well as ordinary employees, former prison inmates, and even former priests and ministers. Now many of them are drug addicts, drunks, demon-possessed, religious-fanatics, prostitutes and homosexuals, many of them with AIDS.

As they eat their sandwich, fruit and desert they tell us their personal story. We then give them spiritual food too, assuring them that there is still hope where they have not yet looked. We talk about the merciful Christ of the New Testament, who loves and still cares for them, and we take them, if they agree, to detox school institutions

Dangerous Dan

like the one I attended myself so they can reenter our society. The number of those who respond is great. Even the authorities of the City of Oakland noticed what we're doing. They officially recognized our ministry and have been helping and supporting us ever since. Praise the Lord!

At the same time Berta and I opened a shop where we collect donations or buy good used clothes and household items, which we in turn sell at very low prices or give them free of charge to carefully picked people and families in need.

Sometimes while looking at the tattoos on the muscles of my arms, I sit back and reflect on how God took from the mire of debauchery a long-term convict and useless person like me, how he cleansed and formed me the way he wanted me to be, and how he still uses me even now, twenty-five years after the episode with my sister, to help others in need; needs like my own in the distant past, and still others of the modern man. Glory be to the name of Jesus! We took only one small step of faith, and He ran to welcome us and bless us with abundant spiritual and material blessings and use us for His glory.

Oakland, California
As I heard the story from the Rev. Danny Martinez

Life from Death Row

*You can't change your life story;
however, you can change yourself.*

I became the person of the day instantly. My story was in the media continuously. I was the "hero" of the news that shocked the world, the "Rodeo Drive jewelry shop robbery." My name was on everyone's lips, because almost all were talking about me. But I was thrown in a prison cell in California, accused for seventeen serious crimes, including three murders, three serious injuries, armed robbery, resisting authority, and kidnapping. The calendar showed 1986, and I was only twenty-two years old! The story of how I got there, however, begins a long time ago in Brooklyn, New York.

My father, who was from the Greek island of Karpathos, married my mother, who was from the city of Sparta, Greece, in an arranged marriage. The wedding took place in Brooklyn in 1957, but the marriage didn't go well. The couple, however, stayed together for twelve years and had two girls and two boys. I am the last child, born in 1964. When I was five years old, our parents divorced. From then, until his death in 1980, I saw my father only sporadically. I wish I had known him better, but it was not easy because he remarried. And so, my mother had to raise four children by herself.

In 1971 my mother suffered a serious accident. Her

Life from Death Row

back was broken, and she had to be hospitalized for six months. From that day forward, her health was fragile, and most of the time she was bed ridden, so she sent me and my sister to a Greek Orthodox boarding school in New York. I felt trapped and abandoned there, and I longed to return home. I finally did return after two troubled years, while my sister stayed there for another two.

I was then only ten and did not appear to be a typical Greek-American kid or even a typical mischievous child. I remember being expelled from school was a frequent event. It was usually due to fighting with other children, petty thefts and telling lies. I also worked hard to find porno magazines because I had an overpowering desire for pornography. I was not just naughty. I was more than untamed, more than a rebel. To put brains in my head, my mother and anyone who could help her would beat me up frequently.

Often she took me to church with her. But I grew tremendously bored listening to prayers, hymns and liturgy in a language I did not understand, and seeing strange ceremonial stuff that made no sense to me. I couldn't wait for the service to be over so that I could get out of there. When my mother saw there was nothing more she could do with me, she decided to send me to her sister in Greece who had no children. She had hoped that my uncle and aunt would manage to tame me, to put me on a straight path and make a right man out of me whom everyone would be proud of.

I arrived in Athens when I was fourteen years old. Immediately, my uncle and aunt showed unprecedented interest in me. It was oppressive in my opinion. They

From Myth to Belief

sent me to a Greek high school and even expected me to be a very good student. I was not a good student at the American high school in New York. How could I be a good student in Greece when I did not write or speak the Greek language as well as my classmates?

Fortunately, my classmates helped me with Greek and I helped them with English language. Even so, I didn't do well at school simply because I did not like school. For my uncle and aunt, however, it was very important that I was a good student, that I always abide by the rules and did not do anything that would embarrass them. And when things did not go as they demanded, they punished me as if with holy wrath, like at home in Brooklyn. All these things created bitterness in my heart, because I thought that I was mistreated. So I disappointed them again, continuing my rebellious life.

In about a year's time I quit high school and enrolled at a technical school, but even this I didn't like. Eighteen months later, my mother arrived in Greece and moved in with me. I also had other relatives in Athens. I hung out with them, went swimming and generally kept company with them. Despite all that, my character did not change for the better. I did not feel happy. Rather I felt imprisoned in Greece and wanted to return to America, where I thought I would be free. The opportunity came when a note to appear for service in the Greek army arrived home. At seventeen, I packed up and returned to America to serve in the American army. In about a year I was enlisted and initially sent to a two-month basic training at Fort Jackson in South Carolina. Then I was moved to Fort Lee in West Virginia from where I was specialized as a battlefield

Life from Death Row

machine operator. But the army life did not please me either.

I was eighteen years old. I was reaching adulthood, and I found myself staying with my brother in Las Vegas. I looked back and took a stock of my childhood. I only saw rubble and debris in my life and the lives of others. And the reason for all of it was my rebellious spirit and my erroneous decisions. I grew up unhappy, and fond memories of my childhood were sporadic at best. I wished I was different – better – that I had grown up like most kids. I was becoming a man, and I did not know who I was and where I was going. I was already very depressed and unhappy. An immense emptiness was inside me and I did not know how it got there or how to fill it. I did not know how to be happy.

In the city of easy money and easier loss, Vegas, I became a waiter at the restaurant of a large hotel-casino, but I quickly discovered I did not like the waiter's profession. I wanted to climb up, but I had no qualifications. So, I quit. I got a job elsewhere, but I was fired. Once more I was hired at some other place but I quit again. I walked the streets of the colorful city disappointed, not only because of my job situation, but also because the rest of my life looked gloomy to me. I lived without purpose, without courage, even without the will to live. Full of sorrow, I constantly asked myself, "What's my purpose in life? Why do I live? Is my life worth living? Should I be alive?"

It was December 1983, and I wandered lonely, deserted and poor at the center of the city of shining wealth. Unbearable despair and frustration oppressed my soul. A cloud obfuscated my mind. Then suicide went through

From Myth to Belief

my mind. As a penultimate solution, I decided to ask my mother for help. So I sold my car and bought a ticket to Greece. My mother received me well and suggested that I stay in Greece and find a job so that I could live quietly like everyone else. But this was not what I was looking for, it was not the reason I had come from America, and it was not the solution for me.

So I bought a Europass (a train ticket), and I started traveling Europe aimlessly. I reached Belgium, sailed over to Dover, U.K., but British immigration turned me back when they discovered that I carried only $20 in my pocket. They thought that because I did not know anyone in England, I might get involved in some kind of crime. Disappointed, I returned to Belgium, climbed up a building, and jumped off to kill myself. I miraculously escaped death and returned to Greece even more disappointed, because I was searching for purpose in my life, and I could not find it anywhere. I was looking for something without knowing what. I was looking not only for some sort of a job, but also for something that would allow me to grow into a successful man. And because I could not find it, I started from that moment on to contemplate seriously a solution that would put an end to all, that is, suicide. And I was only nineteen.

I came back to Athens and immediately searched for the tallest building. I climbed up to the rooftop. I sat and wrote a note and left it right there next to me. I got up, went to the very edge, took a deep breath, and bent my knees, ready to start my jump. At that very moment, I heard a loud and clear voice coming from within me: "Don't do it." Perplexed, I hesitated for a moment, wrestled with

Life from Death Row

myself, and decided to ignore the voice. I started over. Again, I took a deep breath, bent my knees to start my jump. Again, I heard the voice loud and clear: "Don't do it." That voice did not let me kill myself, because this did not happen once or twice, but several times. Every time I started my jump, I heard the same voice very clear and loud coming from within me: "Don't do it." Finally, I turned around, took the note, slowly climbed down the stairs and got out to the street. After this attempt, I decided to try again once more to succeed in life. So I returned to Las Vegas hoping that my brother would help me stand on my own two feet.

My past experience in Las Vegas had taught me that I needed at least a college education if I wanted to get ahead professionally. My plan, therefore, was to find a job and stay at my brother's while going to college. Soon, my brother got angry with me for some reason and threw me out of the house. For the first time in my life, I was homeless, but fortunately a friend took me to his place not long after. Life, however, was not getting better for me. I was disappointed and quickly gave up my plans, without blaming my brother. My roommate, a computer "specialist" suggested that I could make a lot of money quickly by committing a burglary. The chances of catching me, he said, were almost nil. Since I was penniless, I accepted the challenge immediately. And in fact, I committed the burglary successfully without being caught! My pockets were suddenly filled with money. I had money to eat, drink and pay my bills. I even had left over money to lead a comfortable life. For the first time in my life, I saw myself as self-sufficient. I would never again spin around begging

From Myth to Belief

for work, nor would I ever fear getting fired.

I could make a lot of money by doing very little work. For the first time in my life, I did something successfully, something that left me plenty of money. The crime excited me and drew me to it, and not only because of the money. The fact that I had finally found something I was good at satisfied me immensely. It also captivated me that I challenged the risk and I won. So with each and every crime I committed, I became more and more courageous, more and more daring as I focused on perfecting my "art." Soon I considered myself untouchable, elusive. In fact, I had convinced myself that I could take anything I wanted whenever I wanted without being caught, and that I was even the rightful owner of it. And I was proud of my accomplishments. The fact that the money entering my pockets was soon spent unwisely and that I started gradually living the life of the underworld did not bother me at all. Once I was out of money, I had only to commit another burglary so that I'd continue living the criminal's flashy life-style. I knew, of course, that I broke the law, and I felt convicted in my conscience all the more, but eventually I didn't give a dime. I had spent many years trying for a normal job in restaurants and hotels, and I did not manage anything worthwhile. Now I too had the right to enjoy the easy life.

One day, I was finally caught and actually put in jail for seven months. But this incident did not wise me up at all to renounce the life of crime. On the contrary, when I got out, I started stealing and burglarizing and living in lewdness again. Almost everyone I knew at that time was a criminal. All my friends and acquaintances were criminals, known

Life from Death Row

by the police or not. My "business" was doing great until I was caught again and locked in for another three months. Again, however, prison did not rehabilitate me. Instead, I committed my first armed robbery just two weeks after my release. It was one of the most beautiful jewelry stores in Las Vegas, and I felt so proud that I was able to rob it without being caught. After I sold the jewelry in another state, with a head full of pride and plenty of money in my pocket, I arrived in Hollywood, California.

I rented an apartment and started living in the movie-Mecca. It was a dissolute life, shamelessly spending on pleasures. Strange thing though, that this huge amount of money dried up in just four months! So I decided to rob an even bigger, richer, more famous jewelry store than the one in Las Vegas. Deep inside, I was hoping that I would get filthy rich by committing such a huge robbery so that I could be financially independent until my old age.

At the age of twenty-two in 1986, I started exploring Hollywood. I noticed a luxury jewelry store in the famous Rodeo Drive shopping street, which became my next target.

I organized the robbery well in my mind and decided on the day of the assault. Without much detail, I can say that everything went wrong from the start. The police reached the scene of the incident in a flash. In a hall next door, Nancy Reagan, the first lady of the United States, was delivering a speech, and the area was filled with undercover cops. They blockaded the store in seconds, and I was suddenly surrounded by police. So, I decided to turn the armed robbery into kidnapping and negotiate.

I held the staff of the store hostage for some thirteen

From Myth to Belief

and one half hours. Over my negotiations with the police, I realized that I would not get out of there alive, and totally confused, I decided that if they wanted me alive, there ought to be a shoot-out. Eventually, one of the hostages suggested that some of us run away through the back door wrapped in a sheet. We really got out wrapped together under a sheet, but before we entered a car, the police threw incendiary grenades at us that brought us to the ground. They ordered us to stay still. The manager of the store, however, tried to sit up and the police shot him immediately, killing him instantly. Myself and the rest of the hostages were seriously injured. We were transferred immediately to the hospital, I in a police car in which I was treated by the police in such a way that I finally fainted.

    I came to myself the next day in a hospital room with IVs in my arms and feet. I made a valiant attempt to understand why I was tied up in my bed. Two policemen, who entered my room and formally accused me of murder and other crimes of the previous day, brought me back to reality. I remember feeling such guilt and regret that I started crying and apologizing incessantly. The police, however, had no interest in the qualms of my conscience. They just needed to get a detailed statement from me in order to support their charges against me. The feeling of despair came down crushing on me. The lives of three people were lost, and those of so many others, including mine, were destroyed. When my situation improved a week later, they moved me to a prison.

    Then a stream of letters started arriving from people I did not know. They were from all over America, from people who had read or heard or seen the Rodeo Drive

Life from Death Row

robbery in the news. What struck me about the letters was that everyone was interested in me and especially in my "spiritual" health! The common element, without exception, was that they were Christians. I was very impressed by their love that was overflowing out of their writings. They all talked to me about a person as if they all knew him personally, as if he were the best friend of all these people. And they introduced him to me, that I should meet him and become his friend. They told me he loves me and wants to save me and forgive me of my sins so that I do not end up in the hell that I knew I was destined for. Jesus, they all wrote, could save me!

By reading the letters, I started feeling a strong conviction in my heart for my sins. In one of these letters I found a tract with a prayer. It seemed to me that this prayer was written especially for me. In the desperate state I was in, I felt the need to pray. I knelt in the center of my cell and I sincerely prayed this prayer to accept the Lord Jesus Christ, the Son of God, as my Savior. Immediately the heavy burden of my horrific sins and that of my dishonest life (I was only 22 years old!), was lifted over me, and the peace of God which surpasses all understanding filled my heart. I was assured not only that God exists, but that he had heard and had already responded to my prayer. I knew deep inside of me that I was a new man with a new heart, as Scripture says, just because I was united with Jesus Christ, who had just become my savior. For the first time in my life I felt truly free even though I was locked in a prison cell. From absolute despair I arrived to complete happiness with only a sincere prayer to Christ Jesus. The change was a real miracle!

From Myth to Belief

In my statement to the police at the hospital, I had admitted my guilt, readily taking full responsibility for the crimes I had committed. I also admitted my guilt at court even before they picked the jury and the trial started. The only procedure remaining for the court was to determine my punishment: death, or life imprisonment.

My lawyer had assured me that I would be condemned to life imprisonment. But after the wonderful experience I had with Jesus, I knew that even if they condemned me to death, I would go straight to heaven to live with Christ forever in his kingdom the minute I was executed, just like the thief on the cross. That made me happy. Why, I was suddenly free of my eternal shackles, even though I was temporarily bound in a prison cell. Jesus had made me a new creature. Through his wisdom and providence he had allowed me to suddenly start a new life. I, who lived without purpose, without courage, even, without the will to live. I, who only shortly before, full of sorrow had asked myself, "What's my purpose in life? Why do I live? Is my life worth living? Should I be alive?" I, whose soul despair and disappointment oppressed unbearably. I had finally found what I was searching for, that something I did not know what it was. I had found meaning in my life after all. And, where? In Jesus Christ!

I, who until then thought that although God existed, he was indifferent to humans, because there was no other way to explain how wicked people prospered and good people suffered in this world. I, who thought that man was autonomous and lived as best as he could according to his potential, the conditions he was able to create himself, or the given situations he could exploit. I, who only believed

Life from Death Row

in luck and not in a personal relationship between man and God. I suddenly became a child of God! Believe it or not, it's true. I accepted the gift of God only by faith in Christ who died for me and was resurrected and is now at the right hand of the Father mediating for me. Immediately I began reading the Bible they had sent me with thirst and hunger. To this day I continue studying it day by day and gradually understanding the richness of the glory of God, knowing the love of the Father God for man and the savior Christ's substitution on the cross for the sinner.

Perhaps someone could say that I turned to God and religion because I ended up in jail. But the prison is also a small, cruel society. There are several things one can do here, even though it sounds like a paradox. First of all, one can perfect his "art" here. He can even be organized into gangs. He can work out regularly to engage in a sport when he comes out, if he's released. He can get involved in a subject professionally and even become famous like the "Birdman of Alcatraz," Robert F. Stroud. He may get involved in poetry or writing and even be published. Or he can paint, like a Christian friend of mine here, a death-row inmate whose paintings are sold for hundreds of dollars out there in the free world. I could, therefore, get involved with something that I liked. But I found exactly what I was searching for in Christ, even under these circumstances, and I do not regret it even for a minute.

I asked my lawyer if I could send letters to the families of all who lost their lives or were injured in the Rodeo Drive robbery, but he did not allow me. So, as I said, the trial took place not long thereafter. There were seventeen crimes for which I was accused. Despite all the efforts of

From Myth to Belief

my lawyer, and despite the emotional depositions of my family, the jurors sentenced me to death. Big shock for me and my lawyer! Despite this, I decided that I would continue to live a life dedicated to God, even while waiting for death.

Approximately thirteen months after my arrest, I was brought to the famous maximum security prison in San Quentin, California as a death row inmate in July, 1987. One Saturday in 1991, I had the radio on at an unusual time for me. Suddenly, to my great surprise, I heard a program in Greek. I could not believe my ears. *A Greek radio program in the San Francisco Bay Area, in the heart of California?* I wondered. Yes, it was *The Greek Hour of Hope*, the weekly broadcast of the Greeks for Christ Ministry. Immediately I jumped up, jotted down the address and phone number, and sent a letter to the speaker of the show hoping to meet him. He responded himself, offering to come visit me in jail. That gesture of his made a big impression on me. After him, members of the Greek Church in Oakland also visited me. And I wish many more to come often. I keep a very good relationship with them, and I have often given my testimony and spoken by phone to all the believers of the Church as they gather for worship on Sunday mornings. I would say this is my Church. Thank God, indeed, that the Women's Ministry of the Church has repeatedly sent me boxes of sweets, food and necessary personal hygiene items. Many of these I share with other colleagues of mine, so they too are blessed along with me. I also call the offices of the Church often for prayer and support. Glory to God's name for Greeks for Christ!

My life is now limited and simple, but I thank God for

Life from Death Row

all the privileges I enjoy here. Like all colleagues, six hours a day I am free to exercise, to shower, to make phone calls and go to the visiting room if I have guests visiting me. Most important for me, though, is that I have the opportunity to come together with my colleagues who are also believers. We get together almost every day to study the Bible, pray, sing hymns which glorify God and participate in the Holy Communion. We learn that in other prisons Christian believers do not enjoy privileges like these. We are therefore thankful and praise God for all his blessings upon us. I could spend my time fighting with other prisoners, as I did in the old times when I fought everyone while I was out of prison. And it is very easy for anyone to get involved in fights in here, even deadly ones, and many colleagues do, or go searching for them. However, we prefer to do evangelism in our prison. Some laugh at us. If we were in our before-Christ life, they would regret it. But now, we don't mind. We pray even harder for them.

Isn't it great for the criminals of our society to be evangelized and to change for the better? Where else? Even in here! Glory to God's name for it. I also share the love of God with people outside the prison by sending a great deal of letters. I pray continuously, I read a lot, especially religious books, listen to music that glorifies Christ, watch Christian programs on TV and hear *The Greek Hour of Hope* every week. I've also authored three books that I hope will one day be published.

I've been condemned to death in the maximum security prison of San Quentin for about twenty-two years, because my appeals are pending. Along with me there are about

From Myth to Belief

630 others condemned. I do not know whether you can conceive what it is like when at the break of each and every day of your life, there may be a chance that they will come announcing that your life ends in sixty days when you will be executed. But no day passes that I do not have upon me a feeling of protection, peace and the provision of God. His grace and blessings on me are abundant. I praise God for them every day of my life. I intend to continue living for Christ wholeheartedly for as many days as I have left.

There is no need for anyone to come here to meet God. There is no need for anyone to be in prison like me in order to feel like a prisoner. How many people outside of prison walk the walk of life in shackles, as I once did, free people that are prisoners of their own desires, passions, of their overt and hidden sins? How many discouraged people are disenchanted and thinking about death? There is no need for one to lose his freedom in order to understand the value of life. Nor is it necessary to commit crimes in order to feel the love and forgiveness of Christ within. "All are sinners," confirms the Word of God, and I'm the greatest one. My life is a story which I am ashamed of. I am not ashamed, however, that I bent my knees when crushed and accepted Christ's forgiveness. I am very sorry for my life, that I wasted it unwisely. And frankly, I am ashamed even more for those who perished in the Rodeo Drive robbery. I wish I had the power to bring them back to life, to give them back to their families as if nothing had ever happened, as if that horrific crime had never taken place. I wish I could take their place. Now, I am a prisoner and a death row inmate. But I am forgiven. Because Christ died even for me, a criminal! He has forgiven all my sins. The

Word of God in Acts 10:43 says: "…through His (Christ's) name, whoever believes in Him will receive remission of sins." I am convinced that someday I'll see my Savior face to face, because He provided me with eternal life in addition to his forgiveness.

The same forgiveness and eternal life Christ promises to all who believe. "For God so loved the world that He gave His only begotten Son, that whoever believes in Him should not perish but have eternal life" (John 3:16). I'd like to urge you to give Christ first place in your life. God will give you the strength to live responsibly as a free man according to the teaching of the infallible and precious Word of God, the Bible. I believed in him and I trust him. I wish and pray that you too, who read my life story now, believe in him and trust him with your life.

As I heard the story from Steve Livaditis
in an interview at the famous
maximum-security prison San Quentin, California

A Last Wish

> *"He who believes in Me,
> though he may die, he shall live."*
> John 11:25

The grandson of a Greek immigrant, John had two months to live. He called it fate. The parents of his teenage victims called it justice.

Early in April of 1990, John Thanos was paroled eighteen months early by mistake. A career criminal who had spent most of his life behind bars, Thanos went on a Labor Day weekend rampage across central and coastal Maryland. *The Baltimore Sun's* May 17, 1994, issue reported that "he kidnapped and robbed a Salisbury cab driver, shot and killed [a welder who picked him up hitchhiking], wounded a Salisbury convenience store clerk and then executed [a teenage boy] and [his girlfriend]."

On May 17, 1994, at 1:10 am, strapped to a 300 pound steel table in Maryland's Penitentiary, forty-five year old Thanos was put to death by lethal injection. It was Maryland's first execution in thirty-three years.

The front page of *The Sun* characterized John Frederick Thanos as "unrepentant," "remorseless," and an "arrogant murderer." Yet, most did not know that God was dealing with John in his prison cell in Baltimore during the last two months of his life.

The impending execution of John Thanos was

A Last Wish

presented in a USA Today article in the March 9, 1994, issue. Reverend G. Goomas, the Greeks for Christ leader in Dallas, Texas, read the article and sent it to the offices in Oakland, California. Immediately, Dr. Peter followed up by sending a letter for Thanos to the St. Mary's County of Maryland judge, the honorable Marvin Caminets. Finally, on April 18, 1994, John responded:

"Dear Father Peter,

Thank you for your time and offer of spiritual support — your letter alone has fulfilled that spirit and I feel blessed to be thought of kindly. Your assumption that I am Greek is in part accurate. My grandfather came from the old country to the States and then established a family. ...I had a very rich Greek upbringing that is treasured in my memories. The old ways died out as the family split up and died off. ...I wouldn't change a thing in this world, not even my fate scheduled for May 16th. ...Again, your thoughtfulness is a blessing. Will you please send me a New Testament?

Very truly yours, John F. Thanos."

Meanwhile at the Greek church in Oakland, California, and the home churches of the Greeks for Christ Ministry, a prayer war on behalf of John Thanos was going on. Some people also wrote him encouraging letters. A New Testament was sent to him from the offices of the ministry. On Tuesday, May 3, 1994, just two weeks before Thanos was executed, Dr. Peter wrote him another letter:

"Dear John,

You don't know how happy I was to receive your letter. As you wrote, your family kept the Greek traditions. You should know, then, that the ancient

From Myth to Belief

Greeks believed that after death the soul travels through space, shedding every part of man's flesh and blood existence, even his self-consciousness and reason. The ancient Greeks believed in the immortality of the soul but not of the body. For them, the material was evil, and the resurrection of the body an impossibility.

"That's why some of the Athenians mocked the Apostle Paul on Mars Hill, while others said, 'We will hear you again on this matter' (Acts 17:32) when he preached the Resurrection and said that God 'has appointed a day on which He will judge the world in righteousness by the Man whom He has ordained. He has given assurance of this to all by raising Him from the dead' (Acts 17:31).

"Paul's next stop was Corinth, where he expounded on the Resurrection. The Biblical teaching differs from our tradition. Paul said that during the Resurrection of the believers at Christ's Second Coming, our bodies will also come out of the graves; however, they will be glorified bodies. This teaching is found in 1 Corinthians 15:42-44: 'The body is sown in corruption, it is raised in incorruption…it is sown a natural body, it is raised a spiritual body.' The body of the believer will be raised a 'spiritual body' by the Spirit of God.

"In order for the body to be resurrected by the Holy Spirit of God in Christ's Second Coming, the Holy Spirit must dwell inside the body from now, as it reads in Romans 8:23, "…we ourselves groan within ourselves, eagerly waiting for the adoption, the redemption of our body."

"Christ died on the cross in our place. Three days

A Last Wish

later, He rose and said in John 11:25-26, 'I am the Resurrection and the Life. He who believes in Me, though he may die, he shall live, and whoever lives and believes in Me shall never die.'

"Christ's work of redemption offers a twofold blessing: First he saves us by his death and by his shed blood. Whoever repents of his sins and cries to God for forgiveness is promised cleansing of sins by the blood of Jesus. 'The blood of Jesus Christ his son cleanses us from all sin.' (1 John 1:7.) Second, the Holy Spirit is sent by the Lord Jesus Christ in him who is cleansed by his blood. 'I will pray to the father, and he will give you another Comforter, that he may abide with you forever...I will not leave you orphans... Because I live, you shall live also.' (John 14:16-19.)

"My dear John, you can entrust your life and your eternity to Jesus Christ, as I did earlier in my life, in Athens. Don't forget that Jesus was executed, as you will be on May 16. Jesus, however, was different from us, being the sinless son of God! You can ask for the blood of Jesus to cleanse you. God will answer this prayer, and since I will not be able to meet you here on Earth, I look forward with great joy to meeting you on the other side one day."

John Frederick Thanos died on May 17, 1994, having made his peace with God! *The Sun* reported of Thanos on May 17:

"Last week, he told a federal court judge that he believed in an afterlife and would rather go there than spend the rest of his days in prison." Before the execution, Father Chuck Conterna, the prison chaplain, called. "John's last

From Myth to Belief

wish," he told Pastor Peter, "was to thank your church for its help." After the execution, he again told Pastor Peter, "I am so happy to tell you that John died a different man, with much hope and readiness to meet God!"

Maryland, Texas, California

Miracles of Healing

A miracle is an extraordinary supernatural event performed only by the almighty God, the Lord. Jesus said, "With men this is impossible, but with God all things are possible."[1] God is sovereign, and no one can counsel Him what to do. At the same time, God is love, and because of His love and mercy, He performs miracles.

The Bible is replete with miracles. We see examples of such miracles in the Old Testament in the parting and crossing of the Red Sea, the feeding of the hundreds of thousands of Hebrews in the desert for forty years, the protection of the Hebrew young men in the fiery furnace, etc. In the New Testament, we read about the miracles which Jesus performed. For example, turning the water to wine at a wedding in Cana, blind men receiving their sight, deaf men being able to hear. He resurrected Lazarus from the dead after been dead for 4 days. Jesus walked on the water, calmed the storm, fed thousands of people out of a small basket of fish and bread. Jesus even resurrected himself from the dead by the power of the Holy Spirit after been dead for three days, and other such miracles that cannot be numbered.[2] To God, who is beyond the limits of time and space, doing a miracle is normal work, but to us, it is a supernatural event that breaks the Laws of Nature and cannot be explained.

What are the purposes of God's miracles? Mainly to reveal and establish who God is, that He is the almighty God the Lord, who reveals His nature to us, and proves that He is the provider and healer.[3] Miracles prove that God hears and answers prayer.[4]

He assists people in difficult situations; He brings miraculous healing to peoples' bodies and souls, and gives the Holy Spirit to those that trust and invite Jesus into their lives. Miracles that we see in our lives increase our faith in the Lord, and the faith of anyone else who sees these miracles. Miracles fulfill prophesy and establish the validity of God's word. Lastly, miracles confirm that Jesus is the incarnate God and establish His authority. The ultimate purpose of miracles is that we would know God more closely, to trust Him as Lord, to submit and to depend on Him.

In the New Testament, we see that people worshipped the Lord after they experienced a miracle, and others offered praise and thanksgiving. Many people who believed in Jesus repented of their sins and were saved by the grace of God. As a result of just two miracles, thousands of people decided to trust and follow Jesus in their lives (at the Day of Pentecost, and after the miracle of the lame man at the Beautiful Gate).

Jesus is still doing miracles today because He does not change.[5] One of the greatest miracles of God, however, is to watch a new believer's life being transformed (a re-birth) by the Holy Spirit, becoming a new creation.[6]

The three case studies that follow are described by the people that experienced miracles themselves. They illustrate the miraculous power of God after a car accident, with eye injuries, through a cancer that disappeared before surgery, and a horrific fatal accident that transformed the lives of a surviving engaged couple. Each testimony demonstrates that God cares, He is present, He protects, He heals, He performs miracles, and with His loving power, He transforms lives. As a result of accepting the grace and mercy of God and experiencing their miracles, these people came to the Lord and are still serving him many years later. To God be the glory. Amen.

1. Matthew 19:26; 2. John 20:30-31, 21:25; 3. Exodus 15:26; 4. I John 5:14, John 14:13-14; 5. Hebrews 13:8; 6. II Cor. 5:17

John Palassis
Cincinnati, Ohio

John Palassis has led the Christian group 'Apostolic Ministry of Jesus Christ' in Cincinnati since the Lord established it in 1980. The ministry is a mixed group of born-again Greek immigrants, Greek Americans, and Americans.

John is a physical scientist/chemist, with thirty-five years of professional experience, five of which were in the private industry and thirty spent with the National Institute for Occupational Safety and Health (NIOSH) which is under the Centers for Disease Control and Prevention (CDC) for the US Dept. of Health and Human Services. His research work amounts to more than sixty publications which he has authored and co-authored. He has presented his work at over seventy national and international conferences and meetings. John has three Board certifications as a Certified Industrial Hygienist, Certified Safety Professional, and Certified Hazardous Materials Manager.

John has been married to Evelyn (Evangelia) from Chicago for thirty-eight years. They have been blessed by the Lord with four children (now between the ages of thirty-three and thirty-eight), all married, each with their own children and living in Ohio.

Recreating my Face

*There is no way you can study the Bible honestly
and not feel the call of God.
Then your life changes course.*

That particular night, I walked slowly into a nightclub in the city of Allentown, Pennsylvania, just people watching. Suddenly I stopped, awestruck, when I set eyes on the most beautiful face I have ever seen in my life. The face belonged to a beautiful brown-eyed brunette by the name of Serra. The fact that she was Italian and I was Greek, that she was a devout Catholic and I was a hard-nose Orthodox, did not prevent us from leaving later that night in each other's arms.

My name is Costas, and I was born in Naoussa, which is near the biblical city of Berea in Northern Greece. Our family was a good, traditional family, with principles rooted in the Greek Orthodox faith. In the early '70s my father died, and I had to migrate to the State of Pennsylvania in the United States for a better future. When I met Serra, who was a professional nurse, I had a very good job as an engineer in a local factory. We got engaged nine months after the day we met. The day after our engagement, something shocking happened to us that changed our lives.

We were driving west on the quiet and picturesque Highway 22 from the town of Easton to Allentown where

From Myth to Belief

we lived. At exactly 2:35 in the afternoon, we were crossing the Lehigh River overpass. Suddenly we saw a car behind us approaching at a breakneck speed. Before we could react, it rear ended us so violently that both cars took off, passing over the bridge railing, and fell tumbling down 150 feet beneath the bridge. The other car landed upside down on the river bank. Out car suddenly stopped, momentarily suspended between heaven and earth on a strong electrical cable which caught the bumper and stopped our flight. Then the car fell softly on the bank of the river on its wheels. A doctor, who was driving just behind us stopped immediately. Running down, he found the driver of the other car, who was drunk, already dead and us injured. Serra was in extremely critical condition. Five minutes before the accident happened, at 2:30 pm exactly, my mother at home started praying for the protection of the family without knowing why.

The doctors did not give much hope to Serra. Even if they could manage to save her life and assemble her back like a puzzle, they said that the quality of life of my twenty-five year old fiancée would be extremely low. You see, Serra had broken her left leg in two places, her right knee, her right arm and several ribs. Toes and fingers had been dislodged, and she had internal bleeding. From head to toe, she had injuries, bumps and bruises. That strikingly beautiful face which had pulled me like a magnet was not so beautiful anymore. The nose had been broken. The zygomatic bone, the bone in the right cheek, was shattered, and the right eye-movement mechanism had been crushed. Pieces of glass had gotten into both the eyes. Serra had also injured her head so badly that she

Recreating my Face

had a serious brain concussion. Her face was black and blue all over, and her tongue was hanging out, severely severed.

Serra was rushed to the Sacred Heart Hospital in the town of Easton, Pennsylvania, where the heroic efforts of the doctors saved her life. They set the broken legs and arm in plaster, and so she remained motionless in a bed, waiting for surgery and the reconstruction of her face. On top of all this, she also suffered pneumonia and almost died. Even so, she passed through all the danger, and was scheduled for surgery.

Right before the surgery, however, the doctors found that the hematocrit, or her red blood cell count, was low because of internal bleeding. Therefore, they postponed the surgery. This was repeated a few days later. Eventually the doctors managed to stop the internal bleeding. The hematocrit rose to normal, so they scheduled her for surgery for a third time, early the next morning.

While her mother and I left home in a hurry that fateful morning to make it to the hospital before surgery, I'll have Serra continue the story and tell what happened early that morning. It was truly an out-of-this-world experience.

During those days, I was a wreck, not only physically, but also psychologically. My mind was giving birth to many seemingly unanswered questions. 'Why is this happening? Why now that we plan to get married? What will happen now and what will become of me? How will I look? Why would God allow this? Where is God? Is there a God after all?' That night I was extremely uncomfortable. I thought of the surgery, the doctors, the anesthesia, about whether and how much it would hurt, whether the surgery

From Myth to Belief

to reconstruct my face would be successful, and if not, how close to normal they could make it. I even wondered whether the surgery itself would be performed this third time.

To stop my mind from racing, I turned the TV on when at almost dawn. All I managed to do, though, was channel surf continuously. Finally, exhausted, I stopped on a channel I had never watched before. This must have been a religious channel, because the speaker said: "There is no distance in God. Pray with me now."

This "pray with me now," drew my attention. I tried to sit up with no success, but by now I was watching intently. And the speaker went on to repeat: "Pray with me: Jesus, come into my heart now, forgive me of my sins, save me, cleanse me, heal me..." Then I caught myself repeating these same words, "Jesus, come into my heart, forgive me of my sins, save me, cleanse me, heal me..." whispering in the beginning, gradually speaking more confidently, and then in a loud voice meaning each and every word I said. At that moment the speaker (I later learned that his name was Ben Kinslow), whom I had never seen before in my life or on television or anywhere else, stopped, and in a thoughtful way, he said he had a "word of knowledge," a term I was hearing for the first time in my life.

"At this particular moment," he said, "in a hospital bed there is a young woman who watches our program for the first time." He then turned and looked straight into the camera and it was like he was looking into my very eyes and talking straight to me alone. He pointed his finger straight as if only at me and spoke with great confidence

Recreating my Face

as he held the right side of his face with his other hand.

"The zygomatic bone on your right cheek is crushed, and this morning you are scheduled for surgery to reconstruct it. However, God is healing you NOW, at this very moment. The doctors will marvel for this healing." Immediately I realized that the speaker was really talking only to me through the TV.

At that very moment, something like a lightning hit me and fiery waves flooded my entire body. My whole life passed before my eyes rapidly like a movie clip. Suddenly I felt one with my Creator. His presence rushed inside of me, an unprecedented presence of infinite love and bliss. I felt instantly healed and peaceful, not only for my upcoming surgery, but for my whole life. Right there, I gained a new heart and new confidence. I felt like a new woman, created anew, as if reborn. And I also felt sparklingly clean. Right then, I realized that this bed of pain had become a bed of healing for me. Furthermore, not only had God healed me, he had also cleansed me from my sins and saved me. Then I realized that all this was the answer to the prayer I'd prayed a few minutes ago.

I was not interested anymore in what the speaker said. I called the nurse immediately and asked her to call the telephone number on the TV screen. Excitedly I told the person who responded what had happened to me. He praised the Lord and asked me to read Romans 8:28. Because I had not only never read the Bible, but did not even own a Bible (even though I was a Christian!), he read it to me: "All things work together for good to those who love God, to those who are called according to His purpose." He assured me that something wonderful would

From Myth to Belief

come out of all this adventure.

At that very moment (and after a long delay due to traffic jam), my mother and my fiancé rushed into the room only to find me crying. They thought that surgery was postponed again, but I told them about the supernatural experience that I'd had and the "word of knowledge" I had received, that I was healed, and that the doctors "would be dumbfounded with my healing." They looked at each other perplexed and felt relief when the nurses walked in and took me to the operating room.

The surgeons were going to have to cut open my cheek and tediously reconstruct the broken bone with a material like wire netting. The surgery would leave a large scar on my cheek that they would try to fix later with plastic surgery. I would not be able to eat and would have to drink only liquids through a straw for an extended period of time.

Before starting surgery, as always happens in such cases, they took a final X-ray so that the status of the bone be confirmed and so that the surgeons could determine the process of reconstructing it with precision. They were surprised and dumbfounded, however, when they realized the multiple fractures were not there anymore, and the bone was whole like new. The advice the surgeons have written in my medical file, a copy of which is in my personal file at my family doctor's, reads: "there is no need for surgery, because the zygomatic bone was healed during the night." God had indeed performed a miracle and had recreated my face with his own divine hand, the same way he had created the face of the first woman in the good old days, the face of my great-great-great-great-great grandmother Eve. Praise his name! Both physicians and

Recreating my Face

our families really marveled of this healing. And here I will turn to Costas to continue and to finish our story.

Aaaah... that beautiful face I saw nine months ago in a nightclub in Allentown, that face that drove me crazy and which I was madly in love with, the face that I had lost in a bad accident; this same face was suddenly back. The very same one! Except it now shone with joy and happiness. Now my Serra was even more beautiful than before. I couldn't get enough of admiring her face. It is amazing how God brings things about. While he reconstructed the face and the broken nose, restored the mechanism of the right eye that was crushed, while He healed the severed tongue and all injuries from the pieces of glass in the eyes and healed the entire body in a single moment of divine healing, he left her left leg in a cast for sixteen whole months! The reason? So that she would be immobilized enough and would systematically study the Bible.

Serra's miracle was not some incident that happened without a purpose. God wanted something from her and me. He wanted us to study his Word to see what exactly he wanted from us, and to instruct us on how we could be useful to our fellow human beings. And then we wanted us to serve Him. So we began to study the Bible together. As we were studying, he opened my own eyes, and I felt the call of God personally. There was no need to find myself in such a hapless situation like Serra. God loved me, even just as I was. So I dedicated the rest of my life to Him.

Yes, later we got married and started our life together making a family. Doctors who examined Serra after the accident recommended that she not attempt to have children, because she would risk not only her health, but

From Myth to Belief

also her life and the lives of the children. God, however, gave us three healthy daughters, and my wife had no problem whatsoever in pregnancy, nor in giving birth, nor after giving birth.

Professionally, Serra was also not the same person anymore. She was no longer a typical professional. Now far from providing hospital care, she takes care of patients as a registered nurse and provides them with words of comfort. She tells her story, how God intervened in her case, and she assures them that Christ can heal them if they too only believe. I too progressed a lot in my work.

That's when we heard about a ministry in California called Greeks for Christ, the main mission of which is to tell the Greeks that Jesus is not only in heaven, nor did he merely walk the Earth some 2,000 years ago, but he is also here now, alive even though we cannot see him, and that he can save them from their sins, heal them, help them with their everyday problems and the countless adversities they face in foreign lands and in the Fatherland. Whether there is illness in the family, marital problems, children who are involved in drugs, drinking, etc., if business is not doing well and they are in a financial dead end, if they have lost their loved ones, Christ can help. In all this and more, Christ can help. Even if they are only looking for love and peace and meaning in their lives, Christ is there, next to them. The ministry also encourages those who wish to open their homes for gatherings and invite friends, acquaintances and relatives who need Christ. So, we opened our home to anyone in need, and started a home-church the same way the first Christians did in the Acts of the Apostles. We studied the Bible, sang hymns in

Recreating my Face

English and Greek that the ministry supplied us with. We prayed and preached the pure Word of God to those who needed it and wanted to come. It was then that something very important happened to me concerning the critical end times we are in according to Acts of the Apostles 2:17.

It was August 1989 when I had a significant vision. At that time, we'd had quite a gathering in our home in Pennsylvania. I felt God's presence powerfully on my right side, as well as joy and happiness entering and filling my whole being.

I walked through the kitchen going to the room where everyone had gathered for prayer when suddenly I felt my body literally taking off at the speed of light, reaching the heavens and staying there suspended. As I was looking with amazement at the blue around me, a wonderful city appeared in front of me as if from nowhere. Then I heard the voice of the Lord behind me.

"This is The City," he said. "After the Rapture (of the Church), my people will live here." I looked at the city for a few minutes. It was literally an out-of-this-world city with tall buildings of exceptional architectural beauty and surrounded by tall walls, but without residents. And as I wondered, my body returned to the same spot from where I had left in our house. I entered the prayer room and looked at all the people around. The preacher was an Orthodox priest wearing the traditional black kalimafki-hat. Then again I heard the voice of the Lord saying to me, "Very, very, very soon, I am sending many floods on Earth. I want to draw people's attention so that they begin to glorify my name. And very, very, very soon after they stop, I will come to take my faithful to heaven."

From Myth to Belief

Within thirty days, on September 16, 1989, the Eastern U.S. and the West Indies were hit by hurricane Hugo, causing 60 deaths and 7 billion dollars in damage. Since then our planet has experienced the most devastating floods of all time by rain, storms, hurricanes and even tsunamis from earthquakes and other causes, which have claimed millions of lives and hundreds of billion dollars in damage.

Besides the home church, we began a prison ministry. We also opened a Christian coffee house we named Lighthouse Coffeehouse. Later we moved to Florida, near the Greek city Tarpon Springs of Tampa Bay. There we found many great opportunities to talk to fellow Greeks and non-Greeks about Jesus Christ, who can meet their needs today. We've been the representatives of the Greeks for Christ Ministry in the Southeastern States for many years, responding to calls from fellow Greeks on the radio ministry *The Greek Hour of Hope*.

Time went by, things changed, our girls are now married women. One thing is still the same in our lives, however. Our relationship with God through Jesus Christ! We continue to pray and study God's Word daily and share the greatness of the Lord with Greeks and non-Greeks in Pennsylvania, where we returned to live. The fact that Serra has no health problems and a very high quality of life is a great miracle in and of itself. Here I have to underline the fact that long after the surgery, which never happened, we found out that the religious program of divine providence Serra watched that morning before entering the operating room was not a live show, but was video-taped two weeks earlier!

Recreating my Face

Just the fact that Sera and I are alive is still another miracle. The miracles in the lives of people are important, but they are simply miracles. Beyond these, God wants us to not only recognize His divine intervention in our lives, but He also wants us to trust Him throughout our lives. He will lead us where He knows is best for us. And it is He who will lead us to share about Him with others who need to find relief and blessing in their lives and earn a seat next to him forever. Thus, Serra and I pray Jesus will use us as handy tools in the design of His church for reaching the Greeks and all our fellow people.

Pennsylvania, Florida,
As I heard the story from Costas and Serra Tsioukas

Without the Fear of Death

The life of a real Christian reaches the tomb, touches it, caresses it, and bypasses it.

That morning we got into our car early and left our home in Seattle, Washington, for the city of Anacortes. Costas, my fiancé, was driving. I sat beside him while my father and mother sat in the back seat. Suddenly on the highway, the car broke down, went off the road and overturned. All got out of it with only a few bruises. All but me, for my face and body were seriously injured. The most serious was the injury to my right eye. The entire eyeball had come out of the socket completely and hung from the nerve as if on a string. I was rushed to the hospital. I slowly came out of sedation on an operating table, where the surgeons were correcting my face. I heard the doctor speaking to my father.

"You can see for yourself that your daughter has lost her eye."

"Hmmm — yes," agreed my father quietly, and added immediately, "Put it back in."

The doctor looked at him in disbelief, leaned over me and gave me more sedative. After painstaking efforts, they put the eye back into the socket and did the best plastic surgery that could be done in the year 1933 to correct the flesh around the eye and the rest of the facial injuries. It took seventy-five stitches to achieve it. I was lying in a

Without the Fear of Death

hospital bed, and my whole world had turned upside-down in a single moment. So it is that a car crash changes your life completely, if it does not send you into the next world. And now I had lost my eye, so I heard the doctor say. I turned to my fiancé:

"Costas, I lost my eye," I said.

"No, you did not," he responded. Quietly I turned onto my other side and prayed to God in faith.

"Jesus, you healed the blind-from-birth man. You can heal me too and I was not born blind."

Theodore, the husband of my fiancé's sister Doula, was present at the hospital. He had struck up a conversation with the head nurse.

"We shouldn't anticipate anything positive for the young woman's eye," said the nurse at some point.

"There's no need — everything will be fine," replied Theodore, calmly holding up the small New Testament he always carried in his pocket.

I am the only child of immigrant parents from Greece. My mother Marika came from a good old family of distillers in the city of Tripoli, Peloponnese in southern Greece. Their famous wines were very popular at that time in Athens. Marika had two sisters and a brother, Dimitri, who immigrated to America in the late 1800's. He settled with his wife in the city of Butte in the State of Montana.

My father Panayotis came from the province of Epirus in northern Greece. At nineteen he left his young widowed mother and went abroad to America. "As soon as I save $3,000, I am coming back," he assured her. The year was 1903. So he boarded a ship in Piraeus, Greece, as Panayotis, and thirty-five days later he landed in New

From Myth to Belief

York as Pete. Somehow he too found himself in distant Butte and rented a room from Dimitri. He worked hard and by August 1915, he had finally saved $3,000. He put his entire household in two trunks and all his money in an extra large wallet. He was all ready to go back home when Dimitri's sister Marika arrived in Butte.

Pete saw her getting out of the carriage and was awestruck by her beauty. Immediately he went to Dimitri and bluntly asked him, "Do you think your sister would like to be my wife?"

"What do I know?" answered Dimitri in surprise. "Let's go ask her."

"I will pray and give you an answer in the morning!" replied Marika.

That evening before she went to bed, Marika prayed earnestly in front of the shrine. In her sleep she saw her father talking to her and pointing to Pete.

"Marika, take him as your husband."

In November of that same year, they were married. A year later, my mother gave birth to a baby boy they named Bill, who died within four hours from complications. The following year the couple left Butte and settled in the city of Bellingham, Washington. I was born there, two years after my brother Bill. But after a few months, Dimitri, the brother who had brought my mother to America, died within a few days. And although my mother loved my father very much and he loved her too, she missed her family and homeland a lot. So she fell into a deep depression.

At my christening, which took place in the Greek Orthodox Church in Seattle, my mother met a beautiful and austere woman. Her name was in fact Archontoula,

Without the Fear of Death

meaning "a real lady." My mother and Archontoula became good friends right away. Slowly they began sharing plans and secrets like close friends. My mother confided in Archontoula and told her of her melancholy. Archontoula confessed to my mother that she hated anyone she didn't like, but she did not tell her that she also hated herself for all these feelings toward other people. Soon, however, they parted as Archontoula's husband found a job in Oakland, California, and the couple moved away.

Finally we settled in the city of Anacortes, Washington. Life in our family had become very quiet and civilized, without quarrels and shouting. My parents always spoke with love and kindness to each other and to me. My father was a gentle character and a well-read individual. My mother was a very God-fearing woman who practiced everything the Church required. She laid down prostrate in front of the shrine at least once a day, fasted on designated days of the week, kept all of the saints' name-days holidays and did all things a good Greek Christian does. And every night before she went to bed she said all the usual prayers she had been reciting since she was little, from The Lord's Prayer to Kyrie Eleison (Lord have mercy) that I had also learned by heart. Then she climbed into bed with melancholy and deep depression, not just heavy inside her, but also showing clearly on her face. That sad expression of her face when she climbed into bed for another sleepless night has become indelibly etched in my memory.

Oh, mother, how sad is your face, yet you're missing nothing. You've got a good, kind and successful husband with a good business, a strong little daughter, harmony

From Myth to Belief

at home, reputation in society and the church. Why this heavy depression? However, I was growing very confident and proud of my parents.

My father, who had the hands of an artist, had become a first class confectioner. He had opened, therefore, a patisserie business, where he worked along with my mother. I liked to get involved in almost everything in the business. I particularly liked the delicious chocolates my father and mother made so masterfully in various designs and sizes.

One day when I was ten years old, we were all together in the kitchen of the confectionery where I was admiring the amazing works of my father. All of a sudden, my mother asked,

"Panayiotis, will I really go to heaven when I die?"

My father stopped working like he had been struck by a lightning. He looked at her bewildered and asked in return,

"You ask me? What do I know?" He then added, a bit softer to reassure her, "Whatever the priest says. We do what the priest says."

"Yes, but I have so many questions, and I take so many pills," mumbled my mother, showing clearly that her husband's answer did not satisfy her. This incident, however, alarmed me profoundly. Why did my mom, who loved the Church so much, and my dad, who knew everything, not know? Why do mom and dad not know? I wondered, and suddenly, my little world cracked.

Two years of uncertainty passed for me. There was more severe suffering for my mother and hard work for my father. Early one day in 1930, the phone rang. It was Archontoula.

Without the Fear of Death

"Good morning, my friend, Marika," she said. "We have moved back to Seattle. My brother Costas invited us to work in his heating fuel business. Why don't you come over?"

The very next day my mother and I left for Seattle. I still remember the state in which we left the store. My mother was straight-faced as ever, head bowed down, dragging her feet in small, heavy, undecided steps. As soon as we entered Archontoula's house, my mother's sad eyes caught a change on her friend's face. She asked, "What's going on, my friend? I see you changed. I see you smiling, joyous, happy, shining with joy and jubilation. You're not the Archontoula I know. You're another Archontoula. What happened to you in Oakland?"

"My friend, Marika, I have changed indeed. Jesus found me, changed my heart, took out the hatred I had in me and replaced it with His love for everyone, even those I could not stand before. Even my name He's changed. Now, they call me Doula" (which means servant).

"What are you talking about? Which Jesus found you? Did you get lost somewhere in Oakland? Where did you get lost? Tell me!" My mother's questions fell like a downpour upon her friend Doula.

"Well, sit right here next to me and let's take things from the beginning," said Doula showing her the couch she sat in. My mother sat near her, and I next to her.

"When we arrived in Oakland, the neighbors invited us for an 'open-house,'" started Doula. She stopped for a moment and then continued. "There was a Greek lady among the guests, named Mary. That lady made a great impression on me. She had something on her, inside

From Myth to Belief

her, which impressed me tremendously. Her face shone peaceful like an angel's. Whenever her lips uttered a word it was like her mouth dripped honey. She always had a good word of compassion and encouragement to say. Nothing negative about anyone came out of her. As you very well know I did not have all this and I longed much to have it. Furthermore, whatever she said, she said it with authority. Even her movements were graced with a heavenly aura. Her whole personality pulled me like a magnet and simultaneously imposed on me with kindness." "Well, just like you, now," said my mother. "Oh! Thank you," smiled Doula and continued. "I approached her and asked if I could see her in private. When we met she explained to me that when you call on Jesus consciously, He gives you everything he's promised in the Word of God; love, joy, peace, happiness, determination, meaningful life. Because Jesus was not only for the old times. Although he was crucified and died then, he was also resurrected and he is still alive today. Therefore if you believe in Him with all your heart and ask Him to forgive you of sin, He visits and stays with you, bringing with him all these gifts of heaven that are for every forgiven sinner.

'I want all of these,' I pleaded in agony.

'You have only to pray to God that He will give them to you, even now,' she replied with kindness. I did not know what to pray, but this is of no significance to God, for he sees our hearts whether we are honest. I lifted up my eyes and said simply that I believed in Christ with all my heart and that I too wanted His gifts in my life. Right away the terrible burden of bitterness and hatred, the uncertainty of tomorrow, the fear of death; they all left me. The void

Without the Fear of Death

created in me was filled immediately with all the precious gifts of Christ Jesus, love for those I hated before, joy for everything that surrounds me, peace in me for tomorrow and no fear of death. Suddenly my life made sense and I felt happy. The feeling is ineffable and indescribable, the experience is real. I can't make you understand, I can't make you feel it. Nobody can."

As soon as mom heard that her friend Doula was free of the fear of death at last, she barely waited for her to finish the story and asked her, "Can anyone receive what you did?"

"Why, certainly," replied Doula.

"I want this experience to be mine too!" exclaimed my mother.

At that moment Doula's husband, Theodore walked in from work. He sat down and immediately joined the discussion. He asked my mother:

"Marika, do you admit that you are a sinner?"

"Yes," she responded humbly, "I am."

"You responded rightly," agreed Theodore and continued, "because the Bible tells us that 'all have sinned and come short of the glory of God' (Acts 3:23) and that 'the wages of sin is death but the gift of God is eternal life' (Romans 6:23)." Then my mother closed her eyes and prayed right then,

"Holy Father, I come home. I want to join your family and become your own child. I want to enter your kingdom. Forgive my sins and accept me in your family. I want to be happy."

I, who was expecting to hear a prayer like the ones she used to say in front of the shrine every night, was

From Myth to Belief

surprised. "I am not so sure about this. I haven't heard this prayer," I thought. Now, what could a twelve year old girl in the 1930s know about sin, salvation, the forgiveness of God and the meaning of life? I believe, however, that my mother's sincere prayer had an effect on me too. The Holy Spirit was also working in my heart even though I did not understand how.

As soon as she opened her eyes right after this short prayer, my mom was a different person. Her face shone with joy. She got up immediately and it was like pure white wings made her soar over pink clouds. I had never seen my mom joyful like this, so very happy!

"This depression that weighed like a heavy black veil on me has disappeared," she confessed. "I suddenly have answers to all my questions. And I'm not afraid to die now. I have peace in my heart." She went on and on, glorifying God.

Then I cried to myself, because I realized that my mom had entered another family of which I was not a member, and I stayed outside. My mom had entered the family of Christ now, but she left me out. I wanted to enter that family too, to become a member of it. So I prayed asking Jesus to accept me in his family, and I received the assurance that both mom and myself now belonged in the same family: God's family. God gave me strong faith to accept the gift of salvation. This is the most real experience I've ever had in my life, even though I was only twelve years old.

Before going to bed at night, mom took her pills out of her purse. She looked at them smiling. Immediately the nightly routine unfolded before my eyes: the slow movements of the pill-ritual with the sad expression of my

Without the Fear of Death

mother's face. It was in contrast to her happy face tonight.

"No mother. You can't. Don't do it, Mom. Please," I begged her. She turned and looked at me calmly and with kindness.

"I do not need them anymore, sweetheart. Christ has healed me completely." She walked out to the bathroom, emptied the little bottles in the toilet bowl and flushed! She threw the empty bottles in the basket, returned to the room slipped in her bed and slept like a baby. These scenes are etched in my memory too. My mother never took pills again in her life. She never missed a night's sleep the rest of her life either. How could anyone not glorify God for such a miracle?

In a few days, we returned home. I asked mom on the bus, "Mom, what will we tell Dad?"

"I do not know, daughter. God will give us the right words," she replied.

Indeed, once we arrived, Mom entered the store full of smiles and in high spirits, hugging dad and kissing him twice. He was dumbfounded! He stopped what he was doing.

"What's going on? What happened to you?" he asked while rubbing both his cheeks, perplexed.

"Jesus saved me, my dear Panayotis," she responded happily.

"What do you mean 'saved?'" dad replied. "Had you fallen accidentally into the sea in Seattle and someone pulled you out, so you want to say there was a miracle?"

"No, I tell you, no. Christ changed my life," mom insisted.

"Yeah, ok — I see you really changed," my father said,

From Myth to Belief

and he looked at me for a moment as I smiled too.

"What happened in Seattle, daughter?" my father asked, as my mom went back to the little room.

"But, Christ saved us, dad," I answered grinning ear to ear.

"Oh God!" I heard my dad whispering, as he turned to work scratching his head even more perplexed. Soon I heard mom praying for Dad in the little room, that God would make him understand, and I heard dad in the kitchen of the confectionery praying to God to show him whether what happened to mom was good so that he could accept it, or bad if he should try to prevent it. Indeed, in the evening my father noticed that my mother did not take her pills. She stood in front of the shrine and prayed prayers Panayotis had not heard before as he was under the blankets pretending he was fast asleep. At a certain moment mom pulled the covers off of him.

"Panayotis, wake up. Give your heart to Jesus!"

"Let me sleep," he replied, turning over and pulling the blankets back over his head. "I've got to work early tomorrow, I want to sleep."

The next day my dad called Theodore, Doula's husband. She picked it up.

"What did you do to my wife?" he asked her immediately. "Panayiotis, we can't talk these things over the phone," replied she. "Why don't you come over to discuss it," Doula invited. Indeed, Panayiotis went to Seattle. Theodore and Doula explained, but he became even more confused. When he left their home, they gave him a Bible, which he left in a corner of his desk, closed and untouched.

For the next three months, my father was in a stalemate.

Without the Fear of Death

On one hand, he saw the change clear in his wife. She did not take medicine any longer, she slept normally, she worked with enthusiasm, she was all smiles, happy and talkative at home, and also to customers in the shop. Even the business was picking up. He liked all these things. Besides, did he not want his wife to be well? On the other hand, he was afraid all these things were only a passing phase for his wife, or maybe it was just a step before something more serious for my mother. And all this Christian talk he had heard from Theodore, how come he had never heard it in his church? Not knowing what to do, he went for a walk one day just to contemplate all these thoughts. He dropped in at the store of a fellow Greek to chat a bit. The Greek saw him in deep thought and in play-on words told him,

"Poor Panayiotis, The Sours (Theodore and Doula's last name) gave you vinegar to drink. They sang to you not our good Gospel that the priest sings to us, they sang to you a different gospel!"

Immediately my father said a polite goodbye to his good friend and returned home. He sat down at his desk and wrote a letter to the National Herald, the Greek newspaper of New York, requesting a Bible with the stamp of the Patriarchate in Constantinople. Once he received it, he went to his office, opened it, and started comparing it side-by-side and word-for-word to the Bible his friends had given him in Seattle. There he found absolutely no difference.

As he continued, however, through the comparison and study he saw things he had never heard in church. He understood increasingly more that he was not doing what

From Myth to Belief

the Bible said. "How come I am a Christian and I am not doing what the Bible says here?" he wondered. Eventually, he arrived at the last book, Revelation 3:20, where Christ says "Here, I stand at the door and knock. Whoever hears my voice and opens the door, I will enter and will dine with him and he with me." When he arrived there, he could not resist any longer, he underlined it, bowed his head right there in his office and prayed to God,

"Yes, my Lord, I open the door of my heart to you. Come dine with me and stay inside me. Make me your own."

In the following years, the life of our family was truly happy. We began and ended our day in prayer together. Love grew amongst us. Both spiritual and material blessings of the Lord multiplied abundantly on us and in us. I was growing up too, kind and quiet. Costas, Doula's brother, noticed me. I also noticed him. He was young and handsome, with good principles and dedicated to his work. Quickly a romance was woven between us, and he soon asked me to marry him. We got engaged and were preparing feverishly for the wedding. It was during those preparations that the car crash happened, the crash with which I began my story.

Immediately my parents, my fiancé Costas, Theodore and Doula, Mrs. Mary in Oakland, California, the Greek Church in Oakland and all the churches from Los Angeles and New York to Seattle began a prayer battle for me. They prayed fervently to God to perform a miracle so that I would be able to see again. The day after the surgery the doctor came to change the dressing. He asked me to open my eye, but I couldn't. So he helped me by pulling

Without the Fear of Death

gently on the top eyelid of my right eye while keeping the left one cupped with his other hand.

"Oh! I can see," I cried out. And, filled with joy, I added, "Costas sits on the bottom edge of my bed and the nurse is standing next to him." The doctor said nothing, changed the gauze, and left.

In a week he came back to examine me. He removed the gauze, examined with the special little light my eye inside and out, examined if my eyes followed the horizontal and vertical movement of the bulb. All was in order. The surgeon then came and told me with admiration, "I am not responsible for what has happened to your eye. This is a real miracle! This just does not happen, even in a million cases."

I am now eighty-nine years old, and I see perfectly with this eye. There is only a tiny little scar on my upper eyelid so that I always remember, I believe, the miracle God did in my life. My left eye, however, has weakened a lot, so I am not able to drive. It's mysterious the way God works in the lives of his children.

The wedding took place as planned. I went from my father's lap to my husband's arms, as I always like to say. In two years I gave birth to our son Bill. The birth was very difficult and my doctor recommended I be careful not to have another child, because I was in danger. Eighteen years later, however, I had my daughter Constantina, a very easy birth. I am proud of the good children God gave us: Bill, a successful businessman with a son, a handsome man already, and Constantina, a doctor in family counseling with beautiful twin boys.

The family life was and continues to be peaceful and

From Myth to Belief

loving, the way my father's family life used to be. I'm not saying that everything is rosy. But Father God always takes care of us with great concern and affection. It is perhaps a great statement to say that God loves me personally.

This is, however, what's stated in the New Testament. "Believe, and you and your family will be saved" (Acts of the Apostles 16:31). Yes, you will be saved. Saved of everything that pulls you away from God's love, that makes you unhappy. The only condition is to believe. It's so simple yet so difficult sometimes. And it is the only way to find real, pure, unselfish, personal love, hope for the future, meaning in life and confidence for after death. That's exactly what I did when I was a young girl and I have never regretted it.

Developments in transportation have given us many opportunities to travel to the Greek churches in California and worship God there. These developments also gave the opportunity for the Greeks for Christ from Oakland to visit us in Seattle often where we had regular gatherings for many years in our home, which we opened for home church meetings. Countless people attended these meetings and heard of the love of God. Many were those who understood that God could help them through Christ if they asked him today to help, just as he helped people when he was on Earth. And they accepted his invitation.

Seattle, Washington
As I heard the story from Marina Lillas

Medicine for Cancer

*If you want miracles in your life,
walk in faith.*

"I am very sorry to be the bearer of bad news Peggy, but you have cancer…"

There is nothing worse than this greeting from a doctor when you were expecting a simple "good morning." Indeed, the previous evening, three days before New Year's in 1976, I had been rushed to emergency services at St. Rose's Hospital in Hayward, California, with incessant internal bleeding and hemorrhaging. The doctor took my husband aside and told him confidentially,

"In an effort to stop the bleeding, we discovered a large tumor in Peggy's uterus, which, I fear, is cancer. We cut a small part of it out and we sent it in for biopsy. Tomorrow we will know if it is malignant or benign."

Now, early in the morning, the doctor stood before me informing me the tragic news.

"Peggy, the biopsy confirmed my fears. The tumor is indeed malignant and you need to undergo surgery immediately." I lay quietly for a moment before answering him.

"No, doctor. I want to go home and be with my family over the New Years before you operate on me." Surprise and disbelief crossed his face, and he pressed me strongly to reconsider my decision in light of the seriousness of his

From Myth to Belief

findings.

"No," I insisted. "I believe in God, and if He wants to give me my health during these few days, he is able to protect me."

With that settled, he scheduled the operation for January 7, 1976. A few days before the operation, however, I received a call asking me to help organize the wedding of a cousin. I decided to see the doctor and ask for another postponement. Amazed and incredulous, the doctor pleaded with me.

"Your situation is critical. I know what I saw in you." He proceeded to explain that cancer could easily enter through the open-ended blood vessels created during his previous intervention and make things that much worse, even with a metastasis. But I insisted.

"Your life is in your hands," he answered me angrily, "and I am not responsible. Rest assured that if you're not here by the tenth of the month for the surgery, I will send home an ambulance and the police myself to bring you to the hospital."

The poor doctor saw me only as a physician would see his patient. He did not know that I had trusted my entire life in the hands of my Lord Jesus Christ. Nor did he know that many people were praying for me. Not only family, relatives and friends, but the entire Greek Church in Oakland, California were praying for me.

The pastor of the Church had asked anyone who wanted to participate in an effort of fasting and praying, with the singular purpose of my healing, to show up at my home the evening before the surgery. Over fifty people attended the meeting. Towards the end of the prayer

Medicine for Cancer

meeting, the Pastor Dr. Peter laid his hands upon me and all the assembly joined hands and prayed together for my healing in an atmosphere intensified and replete with the Holy Spirit of God's presence.

All of a sudden, I felt like climbing slowly above the assembled people. And I felt like an invisible, powerful arm lifted a very, very heavy cloak from me. Immediately I felt light, free and full of joy. Undoubtedly, it was the touch of the hand of Christ. Just as his hand touched the blind eyes and they saw, he had touched my cancer, and I was cleansed. For the rest of the meeting I sang with the others, and our supplications became a celebration of praise to the Lord.

The next day at the hospital, I was extremely cheerful and smiling. So much, in fact, that the doctor was perplexed. He spent considerable time explaining the surgical procedure he would use, the tumor size to be removed, the chemotherapy I would undergo after surgery, etc. As the nurses took me into the surgery, I thanked God:

"Your will be done in my life. Your name be glorified through this illness of mine and everything else the future will bring." As I was recovering several hours after surgery, I prayed the same prayer.

A few hours later the doctor came. This time he had good news.

"Peggy, you're very lucky..." he began. He hesitated a bit and continued. "You know, we didn't find the smallest trace of cancer. In fact, in the place we had found the large tumor, we now found only a small dry cyst. Peggy, you're very lucky." For the first time in his life, the good doctor came face to face with a miracle, and all he could

From Myth to Belief

do was repeat over and over, "Peggy, you're very lucky."

After a few days, I returned home all smiles. My husband and two teenage children were waiting with open arms to welcome a new wife and mother, because the Lord God had given me anew to my family, my friends and relatives, and to my Church in Oakland who united to pray fervently for my healing. In the days leading up to the surgery, I found solace in Psalm 91 and Hebrews 13:8: "Jesus Christ is the same yesterday, today and forever". I thank Him for his miraculous healing power. He proved true when I trusted him as my Savior, my physician and my close friend.

San Leandro, California
As I heard the story from Panayota-Peggy Babbes

Restoration of Families

A society without family principles is destined to be dissolved sooner or later. The force that connects the correct family emanates from God the Father, who should be the head of the family. Then comes the natural father. When God the Father, prayer and thanksgiving to him do not exist in a family, then the devil and his evil forces find the opportunity to dismantle the family, bringing destruction and death.

Keeping God at the center of the family ensures stability, hope and strength to tackle life. Joy and peace flood it. Miracles happen. Then the family members, collectively and individually, become progressive and productive, lead successful lives and find grace before God, the authorities of the country and their fellow men.

It is well known in this day and age that crime stems from psychological problems, and these problems are usually caused by broken families. In our long history of ministry to these families, we have found that the root of physical and psychological disorders in such people is almost always the collapse of family principles. There was no God in the family and parents were unable to play their role. As a man feels secure in the arms of God, so the child must feel secure in the arms of a godly family.

As you read the stories in this section, notice the role of parents before and after meeting and inviting God into the lives of their families. Any human solution to family problems is temporary. Only solutions that God gives are sustained and constructive.

God has no expiration date. As long as you have breath in you, call upon God and tell him of your need. He will listen and solve the problems in your family. The relationships between the members of your family which have been poisoned will heal. Time, precious family moments and blessings that you have lost will be replenished beyond your expectations.

Tom Mentis
Scottsdale, Arizona

Tom Mentis lives in Scottsdale, Arizona, with his wife Paula. They have been members of the Greeks for Christ Ministry for more than thirty years, participating in teaching and preaching in Greek conferences, writing articles in "Chrisma" magazine and other publications, and maintaining a home church. Married for forty-

nine years, they have three wonderful children who love God and five restless grandchildren. In their ministry, Tom and Paula bring their own close-knit Christian family which is a vital example. They teach that the source of strength, unity and love among its members and to the world is God Himself, and that without him, their family and the families of their children could easily have been broken.

Can a Broken Family Reunite?

The storm in life can be a drag.
But it can make you stronger
if you ask for strength from God.

Tassos came to America from the city of Villia, Attica, outside of Athens to finish his studies. He earned his Master's in Physics and Mathematics. He found a very good job at a Bank in the San Francisco Bay Area, married a nice girl and lived a nice and easy life. He soon had two cute little girls, a large and comfortable home and two cars. He was pleased at how quickly he, an immigrant, had achieved the American dream.

His friend Spyros would talk to him about God, but he cut him off.

"Well, my friend, if God is real, let him appear in front of me now, and then we'll talk." And he would add under his breath, "After all, everything's fine with me and mine. What do I need God for?"

Indeed, everything looked great. The girls grew up happy, attending the best schools in town. His wife took care of the family at home while Tassos worked like a dog. Of course, I've never seen dogs work, except for the Huskies, and I don't know why we say this anyway. Well, Tassos worked from early in the morning till late in the

Can a Broken Family Reunite?

evening so that his children, his wife, his family would lack for nothing. He saw everything going better than well, for Tassos succeeded in whatever he set his hands on. He was the master of his life, even the lives of a few others. He used to say that he was "god."

So, everything seemed to be going very smoothly until one dark day, fifteen years into his marriage. Tassos, now a department director at the Bank, returned home tired from work late that evening. He expected to find a plate of hot food and then a good night's rest as he always did. But for some reason, his wife had not cooked today. "Well then," said Tasos, "fix me a hotdog." He sat at the kitchen table eating his hot-dog and reading his newspaper quietly, when suddenly, his wife who stood quietly by the stove, threw him an ultimatum. In a calm and civilized voice, she said, "You know, Tassos? I want a divorce."

Poor Tassos nearly choked to death. He dropped the hot dog onto his plate. Speechless, he saw his home, his family, his cars, his job, his studies, his American dream; the whole world collapsing, falling on him, crushing and burying him. The end.

Still speechless, and with great effort, he finally got up and went to bed, the half-eaten hotdog still on his plate. All night he could not sleep. He could not understand what had happened or why. He had read somewhere that women who marry young, like his wife, sometimes revolted when the kids grew up. "Was this her problem?" he thought. "Perhaps…"

He spent the next day finding ways to save his marriage, but his wife seemed adamant in showing him the door. He gathered up all his personal belongings in a small suitcase

From Myth to Belief

and arrived at the front door of his friend, Spyros.

Spyros saw his friend livid and exhausted and was alarmed.

"What happened to you, Tassos?"

"My wife — threw me out..." said Tassos.

"WHAT??? Why?? How?" asked Spyros. "Before yesterday you were just fine. What happened?"

Tassos told Spyros the story in two short sentences. "I'm losing my wife, I'm losing my kids, I'm losing my family. I have no idea what's going on around me," Tassos whined.

Spyros and his wife received Tassos with kindness and understanding. Spyros even took the chance to talk to Tassos about God again, to tell Tassos that He was the only chance that Tassos had left. In his desperation, Tassos, who denied the existence of God, asked the forces of good, to show him something, anything. He at least believed that there were some kind of forces of good and evil somewhere. Indeed, that night he had a dream that he was reading a book which contained the answers to all of man's questions.

On Sunday, Spyros took Tassos to the Greek Church in Oakland. There Tassos' eyes were opened, he accepted Jesus and his work on the cross for himself. He asked Jesus to become Lord of his life. Immediately the sadness and pain left him and joy filled his heart, that spontaneous joy that only God can give. Then he felt that he was indeed a Christian and that the statement in his ID card stating he was an Orthodox Christian was absolutely worthless. He realized then that if you do not ask Christ to become Lord and Savior of your life, you cannot be called Christian.

Can a Broken Family Reunite?

By reading that book containing the answers to all man's problems, the Bible, his faith grew stronger. Immediately some wonderful things started happening in his life.

First and foremost, a firm assurance rooted itself in his heart that God would bring his broken family back together again, and that He would reunite them in a wondrous fashion. And immediately he shared his conviction with his friends in this way: "God told me that my family would be reunited."

His friends shook their heads as they tried to understand, accepting that Tassos cared for his family, his wife and children to be together again so much that this made him hope, if not simply dream it. The result of this unmovable conviction was that an infinite peace overcame him, and it caused others to wonder.

Immediate interest and deep love for others who were unhappy away from Christ nestled inside him as well. He decided to speak to whoever wanted to hear, even to people in the most difficult situations, about Christ and the peace He is able to give. Not only did he talk to neighbors and acquaintances, but he became active in the Greek Church of Oakland, the local chapters of the Christian Businessmen Fellowship, the Greek Orthodox churches in the area and any place where he found people hungry to hear God's word. Never before had he imagined that one day he would be involved in religious things or that he would be witnessing for God. But he did. He would find Greeks, Americans, foreigners of any nationality, to speak to them of the love of God, of how God is able to change any man, of how God fills the void within themselves, and gives meaning to their lives. And he always reminded

From Myth to Belief

those who knew him, and even those asking about his family for the first time, that God will soon reunite them.

Tassos traveled outside the San Francisco Bay Area, even outside of America, to find people who wanted to hear about God's love. At first, he traveled to Greece and visited his father's family in Villia. They found him changed. He had no trouble at all telling them what had happened to him. They listened attentively, and a great salvation took place in that home and in the homes of his relatives.

After visiting Greece, he participated in several missions to Russia and former Soviet countries immediately after the iron curtain fell. He found people suffering in physical and spiritual poverty and, being ready and eager to hear a few words of consolation from God, they drank it up like dry sponges. After each trip he'd come back to the Greek Church in Oakland to tell the glorious stories and the wonderful things God was doing during his long trips as he prayed and preached to people about God.

He also broadcasted his experiences on The Greek Hour of Hope radio program of the Greeks for Christ Ministry. He did all these things with urgency, as though he did not have enough time left. And he always reminded everyone that God would reunite his family. His friends were so used to listening about the reunification of his family that they did not pay much attention to his persistence on this issue. His girls had grown up and his ex-wife was still unmarried and living with the daughters.

Then something strange started happening to Tassos. Suddenly, he started forgetting things. After a short time, his memory would come back. At first neither he nor his

Can a Broken Family Reunite?

friends paid any attention, because occasionally forgetting things could be normal for anyone, especially someone who was fifty, like Tassos. The forgetfulness, however, continued to grow stronger as time passed. Finally Tassos decided to visit a specialist. An MRI showed that Tassos had a brain tumor that was pushing on the memory center of his brain, causing him to gradually lose his memory. The biopsy results showed that the tumor was malignant. Tassos needed an operation urgently.

This incident sent something like an earthquake through acquaintances, friends, the Greek Church of Oakland and his family. They all surrounded him with compassion and concern.

And finally, his family rallied around him. Yes, his wife and his two daughters surrounded him with love! Everyone started praying for the healing of Tassos, but even more for the healing of his family. Tassos then had the opportunity to witness to every member of his family about the faith he had found in Christ after the breakup with his wife. First, the younger daughter made Christ Lord of her life. His wife followed. Finally, the older daughter responded to a sermon she heard at the Greek Church in Oakland. The preaching of the Word touched her soul and she made a step of faith accepting the work of Christ on the cross and devoting herself to God.

During his long illness, Tassos never complained. He was always happy, positive and upbeat, even before a surgery; and there were several surgeries. Shortly after each surgery, he would get out of bed, glorify God and walk out happy to share the greatness of God with people ready to listen. His wife wondered where he found all

From Myth to Belief

this joy, strength, courage, laughter, positive energy and persuasive words. She also wondered about the radical change that had happened to her husband. Shortly before leaving Earth to meet his Savior Jesus whom he loved more than anything in the world, Tassos held the hands of his wife and daughters. He thanked God, for in His unfathomable wisdom and grace, He not only reunited Tassos' family on Earth, but He also allowed them to reunite in heaven forever.

San Ramon California
As I heard the story from Tassos Tzavaras.
Note: The younger daughter Daphne, a professional soprano, has been involved in the Music Ministry and the CDs published by "Orama Music." The older daughter Elena works as a secretary at a church of the San Francisco Bay Area.

The Claim Letter that was Never Delivered

"I didn't have a customer who wasn't a friend, and I didn't have a friend who wasn't a customer!"

My name is Evangelos Demetrios Marmarellis, also known as Angelo James Marmarellis. I'm a first generation Greek-American. My father came from Pergamos of Asia Minor, and my mother came from the island of Samos.

We were rich! When I was a child, we lived uptown in what was then known as a very fashionable section of upper Manhattan called the Bronx. My father was a wholesale grocer with a fine reputation. A large, strong and very worldly man, I feared and loved him as a child. The year was 1922, and I made my appearance into this world preceded by three brothers. My mother, Georgia, and I almost didn't make it, as she was weak and exhausted from caring for a large house, a demanding husband and three active kids. To compensate for this my father hired a housekeeper to assist my mother.

It was this person who influenced my mother's life from that moment on. The housekeeper was a very godly person who loved the Lord and got my mother to read her Greek New Testament every day, morning and night, in a small closet with a lit votive candle and a picture of the Virgin Mary and the Christ child. My mother's faith in God

From Myth to Belief

was supreme and never wavered through the years.

And then, suddenly, we were poor! The Great Depression of 1929 came and my dad lost his business, his friends and his wealth, estimated in those years at around half a million dollars. We were forced to move to Astoria, New York, at the time a suburban, middle class community comprised of many ethnic groups. My friends at the time were Scotch, Irish, Italians, Jews and Hungarians. It was quite a mixture, and we all got along well.

My dad was most influential in the first Greek Church in Astoria, which was called St. Athanasios and later became St. Demetrios. It is now the largest Greek community, I believe, in North America and boasts its own private schools. I went to public school in Astoria and on to high school. My father went back into business with his older brother, Stephanos, and opened a Greek food market called Marmarellis Bros. on Eighth Avenue in New York City. The Depression soon ended and business was good. In 1936, I graduated from William Cullen Bryant High School with honors. I always worked, even as a child, at my dad's store on weekends. I have pleasant memories of my years there, delivering orders, waiting on people and listening to my father talk to his customers in seven different languages. The amazing variety of people, languages and cultures always excited me.

Then the war came, and I wound up in a defense plant on the night shift. I was subsequently drafted into the Air Force in 1943 and served as a non-commissioned officer in the South Pacific area. My title was Supply Srgt., and my duties were to outfit and equip 186 of my men and about 60 specialists on detached service with us. We were a Signal

The Claim Letter that was Never Delivered

Supply Depot Aviation company first in Guadalcanal, and then in New Guinea. Most of the men were Southerners and Midwesterners, and we lived in tents.

My best friend was a Catholic named Frank. He tried to get me to attend Catholic services, but didn't succeed. Someone gave me a Jehovah's Witness Bible, but I couldn't get very interested in it. I didn't even understand the Greek Orthodox religion into which I was born and raised. I was actually the first altar boy in the Astoria church and practically knew the rituals by heart. During my public school days, I went to Greek school three times a week at the church. As a matter of fact, my older brother Jerry was most instrumental in building two Greek churches, one on Long Island called St. Paul's and the other in Florida. I guess you could call us "good Greeks."

I came back from the army in 1946 and went back to work with my father. My father suffered a heart attack, so I stayed at the store with my uncle Steve, my dad's partner. We got along very well. It was then decided that we should sell the store and that I should join my father in a new business, but this never materialized. My dad didn't recover, and I fell in love with a customer's daughter at first sight. Her name was Mary Savaris. She soon became Mary Marmarellis, and we moved into a new house in Astoria with my brother-in-law and her parents. We each had our own apartment in the same house and got along extremely well. My in-laws were also from Asia Minor and were very helpful in the early years of our marriage. I went to Long Island University on the GI Bill, then to Brooklyn Law School, and finally finished up with a degree from Blackstone Law School.

From Myth to Belief

I worked as an insurance agent for John Hancock Mutual Life during the day and studied law at night. We had two wonderful daughters, Julie and Jean, and we enrolled them at the private Greek school of St. Demetrios in Astoria.

Meanwhile, I left the insurance company and became an independent agent. I owned and operated my business with the help of my wife; an insurance brokerage business called Gem Agency. I was successful, enjoyed the business, and my clientele was almost completely all Greek. I soon joined the AHEPA, the Masons, the Kiwanis and a variety of trade associations. I was busy, very busy. I wasn't home in the evening most of the time. I was always out on business and there was plenty of it, what with car insurance, house insurance, business insurance, jewelry and fur insurance, etc. I didn't have a customer who wasn't a friend and I didn't have a friend who wasn't a customer! Adding to this, I worked as a field brokerage manager for two different firms on Madison Avenue for about eight years while building my own business on Long Island.

Business prospered. My customers never failed to refer new customers to me. Astoria became full of new people, mostly Greeks, as well as Spaniards and other ethnicities. I moved the family to Glen Rock, New Jersey, sold my business on a contingency basis with a reliable firm and opened up a small office. I became a general agent for Sun Life and divided my time between New York and New Jersey. It went well for a while. My girls enjoyed the suburban life and the fine schools. We enjoyed the good life. My older daughter went to college to become a

The Claim Letter that was Never Delivered

teacher, and my younger fell in love with a client of mine, as it had happened years ago with me.

And then it happened: Julie had an accident in the brand new car I bought her for school. She told me she was parked while attending a "religious" meeting at a Presbyterian church. In fact, a busy pastor by the name of Malcolm Smith had hit the car by backing out of his parking space after the meeting. He had been the main speaker that night. He was nice enough to leave his card on her windshield, saying he was responsible for the damage. I got the card, went to my office and had my secretary write up a firm claim letter. Damage was estimated at $246.00. At that time in my life, I didn't know the difference between a pastor and a priest!

My impression of that pastor was that he looked much like a Greek priest: black clothes and a beard to match. I had no use for priests. A product of the early twenties and thirties, I admired the self-made man, the highly educated man, the guy who did it on his own! Like Frank Sinatra, "I did it my way!" In fact, since the church was in the town next to mine, I put the letter in my suit pocket thinking I would deliver it personally to that "black-frocked" religious man.

I got to the church the next morning about 9:15 AM and heard singing. I asked a man at the door for Malcolm Smith. He opened the door slightly and told me that was he on the dais and had just started to preach. Smith was dressed in a fine suit like me. I swallowed hard. "What's this?" I asked the man at the door again. "It's a Full Gospel Business Men's meeting," he responded. My first impulse was to leave and return the next morning, but the words

From Myth to Belief

"business men's" got me. 'How come I don't know this business club?' I thought. I decided to stay for a short while at least. I looked inside the main premises: it was full of well-dressed men and women holding bibles. I wondered why these people weren't at work like everyone else. Then I heard the word "blood, ...the blood of the animals slain for the atonement of sin." My interest was stirred. I noticed one single, empty seat next to the wall on the right side. There were at least one hundred people in that room. I looked at the seat, then thought, "I'd be out of place here, I don't belong here and should go back to my office. I have plenty of work waiting for me. I'd be wasting my time to stick around." So I left. The very next day, I went back, saying to myself, "This time I'll get there early and nail the preacher."

To my surprise, the meeting was already in progress, and again this Malcolm Smith was preaching on the blood. Again, I looked inside and again I saw a single seat in the far aisle. I broke into a sweat as I really wanted to leave for the second time, but the empty seat drew me like a magnet, so I went and sat down next to a woman.

I listened, and then I cried. I cried aloud and everyone must have heard me, I'm sure. Malcolm Smith kept preaching on the blood, and I sobbed and sobbed. I tried to get up and leave, my tears kept falling on my well-shined shoes, but my feet wouldn't leave the floor! I tried to get my body up, but it was no use. It was no use. I just sat there and sobbed, and nobody looked at me, although I'm sure they all heard me.

Malcolm Smith never dropped a word, he just continued on. Finally it was all over. The woman next to me got

The Claim Letter that was Never Delivered

up and joined hands with me as everyone sang Rock of Ages. It was only then I realized that the Rock they sang about was Jesus. I went back to my office in a daze, not realizing that once more, I hadn't give Malcolm Smith the claim letter for the damages. I drank three cups of coffee and tried to figure out what had happened to me. I decided to have my secretary send the letter out to Malcolm Smith for me. However, the next day, being Friday and last day of the meetings, I decided to go again, not realizing I had a rendezvous with the Lord.

To my surprise, Malcolm Smith was not there, but Clare Hutchings, an evangelist, was. He preached on salvation, invited people to go forward, laid hands on them. People fell down. An exorcism took place, and a demon was cast out of a young woman. It was an amazing sight. I had never seen anything like it. He made a final altar call for salvation, and I found myself in front of him; he touched me, and then He touched me. I came to the Lord, and to this day, I can't sing He Touched Me without crying.

I went back to my office, the claim letter forgotten in my suit pocket, drank another three cups of coffee and left for the nearest bookstore to buy a $30.00 Bible. I devoured it every day, even neglecting my work. I wanted more of the Spirit. About a week later I dropped my wife at her department store on Route 4 in New Jersey where she was Assistant Buyer, and instead of going to my office, I went back to the house. I got on my knees in front of our bed, opened the Bible, and began to read from the book of Isaiah. I raised my right hand the way my mother used to in front of the icon of the Virgin Mary and the Christ child, and with the open Bible in my left hand, I cried for the Holy

From Myth to Belief

Spirit to fill me, my eyes full of tears and my mouth reading. And suddenly, He came. The words poured out of me in what I thought it was English, but it was another language. I was stunned, my lips felt on fire, I spoke again in English, and again the words seem to be like Arabic. I had heard it many times in my dad's store. I spoke for about twenty minutes. I spoke English, but the words came out foreign again. Very few people know about this and I have kept it private, but now it must be told.

Soon thereafter, my wife, my daughters and my three grandchildren were also born again. But the story doesn't end there.

The Lord soon led my wife and me to go West now that one daughter was married and the other had become a schoolteacher. So, selling our New Jersey home, we left everything behind and went to New Mexico. First we became active in the Full Gospel Business Men's organization, then with the Greeks for Christ Ministry, and then the Gideons, placing Bibles in hotel rooms, hospitals and schools. We also helped build a church in our town, sponsored missions in Africa and have supported various ministries for the past thirty years.

We've gone through some rough times here in New Mexico, but the Lord pulled us through every one of them. Praise His name! We've seen miracle after miracle in our lives, even to this day as we're in the Word daily. I will tell you one worth mentioning.

One Friday evening, three months after we arrived in New Mexico, we were very tired and didn't want to drive some thirty miles away to attend a meeting. However, I became ill at ease and, though unshaven, felt impressed

The Claim Letter that was Never Delivered

by the Lord that we should attend. I thought, "We'll go all right, but we'll sit all the way in the back of the meeting room and no one will see us." To my surprise, we were noticed, and the leader pointed to me and asked us if we would come up and give a witness. I gave my testimony as briefly as I could, and then Mary, who never spoken to an audience before in her life, also spoke. I hardly remember what she said, but a fine, dapper looking gentleman later started changing seats till he got near us. We were introduced. The next morning we went again. Again this man came to us. He was a Catholic. I boldly asked him if he was born again and if he knew the Lord. I prayed the sinner's prayer with him. His head was about on my right shoulder, and then it happened.

I asked him if he had been a Marine in WWII. He said yes. I asked if he was now a barber. He said yes. Then I asked him if he was going to commit suicide last evening when he met us. Again he said yes, and collapsed in my arms. I gave him a little Gideon New Testament I had. We took him to the house that day at noon and we had prayer and lunch together. When I heard from him again not long thereafter, he was at a hospital in Albuquerque witnessing to Catholic nuns. He could never talk to my wife on the phone without crying. Isn't it wonderful to see men and women being saved from death, being filled with life and becoming useful to other people? God is so good to the children of men!

It is of great importance how the Lord takes advantage of circumstances to approach people and give them an opportunity to change their life, improving it on Earth as well as in Eternity. In my case, He used a car accident

From Myth to Belief

and a claim letter that was never delivered. Now, born again and blood-bought, we look forward to his coming. Hallelujah and Amen!

Santa Fe, New Mexico
As I heard the story from Angelo Marmarellis

Something Wonderful will Happen to You!

The devil sees only upside-down things the way they are.
Everything else he sees upside-down.

The ship on which I worked as a second engineer was in the middle of the Atlantic Ocean. We were sailing from Amsterdam, Netherlands, to Montreal, Canada, when a tremendous explosion in the engine chambers shook the entire ship. I was on duty at that time and was severely wounded. Among other things, my arm was cut opened so deep and wide that the bone was clearly visible. The blood gushed in a torrent. My colleagues did everything they could to save me, but I was quickly losing both my blood and my consciousness. I couldn't see or hear anything around me, and I realized that I was slowly dying.

My whole life passed before my eyes in a rapid succession. Then a little voice whispered to me, as if in the ear, "Do not worry, Peter. *Something wonderful will happen to you!*" Even though in a daze, I realized that this was no human voice. I think this voice kept me alive by giving me hope. Shortly after that, I fell into a coma. Seven more days passed before we finally anchored in Montreal, where they rushed me to an emergency hospital. The doctors fought an epic battle to save my life, as they told me later, for I was still unconscious. It was 1966.

From Myth to Belief

I was born into a proud Greek Christian family in Cairo, Egypt, at the end of World War II. We had a nice house with servants and many other conveniences, because we had lots of money. My father, who was from the Greek island of Leros, worked as chief engineer for Shell Oil Company in Cairo. He believed in God, but he never went to church except to marry and baptize his children.

My mother was from the Greek island of Samos and bore for him two sons and three daughters. She too believed in God and went to church from time to time. Still, my parents sent us children to Agia Triada Church regularly. They also sent us to the private Michaliades Brother's Greek school.

All of those in our family believed, like all Greeks do, that we were born with the Orthodox religion under our skin. Now whether or not we practiced it was at our discretion, and in fact, we did not practice it, because we did not consider it necessary in our lives. It is no exaggeration to say that I had never seen a Bible in my life. I had never read a single chapter. I did not know the message of God's love for man at all, and did not really believe that Jesus died and actually rose from the dead. I had always thought, like many others, he was one of many good teachers who was killed by the Jews.

When I was six years old, I remember, riots erupted in Egypt. Members of a revolutionary organization, called The Muslim Brotherhood arrived late one evening outside our house. They began swearing at us and marking seven crosses on the walls of the house using chalk, which meant that there were seven Christians in the house, my parents and five children. We children ran fearfully away, grabbing

Something Wonderful will Happen to You!

the pant legs and dress hems of my father and mother. My parents tried to calm us down by reassuring us that everything was ok.

   Shortly after the raiders had left and the neighborhood was once again quiet, my mother went out, and, with great courage, she cautiously erased the crosses. We did not sleep a wink during that night of anguish. In the morning we found out that many Armenian Christian and Coptic Christian families were massacred during that terrible night. The killings in Cairo were followed by riots and looting against Christians caused by a small number of Muslin extremists. Those incidents were condemned by the majority of Muslims most of whom were innocent people and many of them were our friends. Nevertheless, they did nothing to prevent it. Thus from an early age, I learned to live in a dangerous environment.

   Fortunately, my father found a better job in Suez four years later. My family moved into an even bigger house supplied by the new company. It was in a better neighborhood and had even more servants. We liked it so much that we thought we would live there forever.

   On an October morning in 1956, not even a year later, we heard gun fire and commotion outside of the Greek school in Suez. There was shouting from soldiers in the streets that *the Israelis were coming*. Soon soldiers walked into the school and told us to leave immediately, because they were going to install anti-aircraft guns on the roof. We left the school in panic, and when we came home late that night, we found it occupied by soldiers! They ordered us to leave our house too, because the Israelis were coming. They continued to emphasize this phrase.

From Myth to Belief

They herded us onto a military truck and sent us to Cairo, ousted from our home and carrying only two or three suitcases and the golden rings on our parents' fingers. All of our assets, bank deposits, gold, silver, expensive household items and other riches, we left behind in Suez. All this became property of the Egyptian government since President Nasser nationalized everything in Egypt that day, including the work of my father. However, the authorities proposed that if we were to become Muslim Egyptian citizens, they would return our entire property intact. We rejected that proposal immediately, as did all of the other one million Greeks in Egypt, half of which were in Cairo, one hundred thousand in Suez and so on.

My father could not find a job in Cairo either, so we left for Alexandria. From there, impoverished and penniless, we boarded the first boat we found for motherland Greece, the only hope we had left. Very few people know what the Greeks of Egypt had had and lost when we were thrown out of our homes and country. Vast arable land (i.e. cotton fields), great factories, giant retail stores, huge fortunes; all were left behind, lost overnight.

We arrived at the port of Piraeus in February 1957 and immediately sailed to Rhodes, where we had some distant relatives. They welcomed us and gave us a tiny run-down room so at least we could put a roof over our heads. The entire seven-member family stayed in one room. On a cold and rainy night just a month later, an earthquake struck. Along with the other panicked people of the city, we ran out of our collapsed houses in the dark and in our pajamas. Our room had collapsed. Stuck on the crumbling wall, we tried to avoid the rain. We stayed there all night. We

Something Wonderful will Happen to You!

stayed there the following day which was dark with heavy clouds, and then the next night. Our relatives also lost their homes and could not do anything for us. People who passed by looked sorry for us and went on to their way without a word, without doing anything to help us.

At some point during this time, an endless shining black limo turned the corner of the street slowly, drove even slower in front of us. The window of the back seat rolled down slowly. An elderly hand with a heavy precious ring appeared to be doing the sign of the cross, blessing us. The hand was pulled back in the limo, the window was rolled up, and the local bishop in his stretch limo drove off as solemnly as he had come. Speechless, I turned and looked at my father. It was the only time in my life I had seen him cry! Was this the better life we were to find in our Christian homeland Greece, leaving the Muslim country of Egypt?

The next morning a stranger came and talked to my father in broken Greek. I saw my father nodding in an agreeable manner, and turning to us, he ordered us to follow them. The stranger, our angel of goodness, took us to his home. He gave us food to eat, water to drink and a place to sleep next to his own family. Later we learned that this stranger was an elementary school teacher and a Turk!

A week later, tents from the royal provision arrived, so we moved into one and stayed for six months. We also received a gallon of soup and one half pound of bread per family per day. I was so hungry I started praying desperately to God to provide us food to eat.

I managed to finish junior high school and then attended

From Myth to Belief

a four-year public school of naval engineers called Nereus. I graduated as a merchant marine engineer. At the age of nineteen, with a good degree in my hands, I got a job with merchant ships and began to travel around the world. I was in a port in Los Angeles at two o'clock in the morning when a Greek immigrant from the Greek Church of Los Angeles named Emmanuel Maragkakis came to our ship to visit us.

Emmanuel carried a large bag of Bibles in the everyday Greek language to give to everyone in the ship. He gave one to me and talked to me about Christ. He told me about His love for me and about how Jesus had eternal life to offer me if I believed. I just smiled sarcastically, considering him a heretic and wondering if someone had paid him to convert us. I found it impossible to accept that this Greek was a real Christian and that he loved his fellow countrymen so much that he sacrificed his sleep, time and money to visit and talk to them about Jesus. He even invited me to church to hear the Word of God, and he was so good and convincing that I could not refuse.

The next day was July 4, Independence Day in the US. The year was 1969. So I went to church. I listened to the sermon and a miracle happened to me. First, I realized that I was a sinner. Second, I believed that Christ could save me and change my life. Third, I knelt before God and asked him in prayer to accept me the way I was. Indeed, as soon as I finished praying, my whole life was changed. The vague notions about God, my distorted opinion about the world, my blurred plans for the future, everything had turned around and become so real as to have taken flesh and bones. My world had been turned upside down by

Something Wonderful will Happen to You!

the devil, but God suddenly came into picture and turned it right side up.

At that very moment, I knew without a doubt that Jesus was alive. He not only performed this miracle in me, but also gave me eternal life, just because I accepted through faith his death on the cross for me and his resurrection. Right then and there, that little voice I had heard when I thought I was dying in the middle of the Atlantic Ocean, that same voice came to me again and said, "Peter, this is the wonderful thing I promised you." I knew beyond a shadow of a doubt that this was the sweet voice of God himself. True joy and peace flooded through me, and they have never left.

Two years later while praying, I felt a fire burning me inside without pain, and immediately I heard myself glorifying God in a language I do not speak or know. This is the touch of the Holy Spirit (Acts 2:1-4), which God supplies to those who request it.

Later I found in the book of Hebrews the following passage: "God sends his angels to protect those who will be saved" (chapter 1:14). Neither the massacre in Suez, nor the earthquake in Rhodes, nor the accident in the Atlantic Ocean could kill me, because God had a plan for me. Later in life, I saw the hand of God helping, protecting and giving me courage throughout my life. One thing is certain, that Christ is real, just as he is presented in the New Testament. He died and was resurrected after three days and now supplies salvation, healing, protection and all his gifts to anyone who requests them.

Never before had I imagined that I would find a companion in life who agreed with me so completely. But

From Myth to Belief

in 1974, God gave me a very faithful woman with whom I have built a Christian family that loves and serves God. Both our daughters have married men who really love God and our son is to marry a strong Christian woman too. God's blessings and goodness to me, a forgiven sinner, is above human understanding and beyond all expectations. The only thing I can do is lift my hands up to Him and constantly give my biggest thank you.

And one last thing. Today I am the pastor of the Greek Churchin Los Angeles where I first met Jesus when I visited on July 4, 1969.

Los Angeles, California
As I heard the story from the Rev. Peter Fylakouridis

The World Champion Who was "Resurrected"

"When I am weak, then I am strong."
2 Corinthians 12:10

Elias, a world heavyweight wrestling champion for more than 40 years, was famous in Australia, where he lived with his family. He was famous in Greece and the whole wide world. He was lucky because his street smart, active and hard working wife was also his manager.

The life of brawny Elias started in obscurity and want in Greece. He worked hard and practiced endless hours until he became a world champion. He wrestled famous Greek and foreign wrestlers like Karpozilos, Kapaflis, Lamprakis, Primo Carnerra and countless others. He was mild mannered and he never boasted of his fame. As a matter of fact, he used to say, "Hard work always keeps one in shape, regardless of his age." He proved this saying true, as he was strong and powerful even in his ninth decade of his life.

On the contrary, Maureen, his wife started her life in a colorful way. She was born into a family of musicians in New Zealand. At the age of seven, she performed on stage at big theaters along with her older sister. For several years they sang and danced together as a team in many theaters of their country. Later, even though they

From Myth to Belief

were very young, they formed their own theatre company and became famous, touring New Zealand repeatedly. The feeling they felt from the applause of their fans was indescribable. People generally believe actors and singers are the happiest people on earth. Yep, the sisters were! That is, until they walked off the stage. When they arrived home after a performance, they drank themselves unconscious to drown the feeling of emptiness that was left when the clapping and enthusiasm ceased.

Their parents' quality of life was not better either. They attended party after party thrown by their colleagues and arrived home already drunk at night. There was no one to care for the children who grew up separate and independent. Practically, the family was broken. Eventually the elder sister got bored with this and made her exit by getting married. Maureen then left for Australia alone at the age of sixteen, where she continued her artistic career. After ten troubled years, she met Elias in Sidney, whom she married. Together they began a truly glorious career: He as a wrestling star and she, his able manager.

Their lifestyle became one of continuous success with popular wrestling matches, adoring fans, social events, public relations and appearances, invitations from admirers and opponents and non-stop traveling. They were always surrounded by friends. It was life in the fast lane. Their family life also was harmonious as well. They were a happy family, a blissful couple with three lovely children, a brand new, wonderful, expensive, huge house, expensive cars and plenty of money in the bank. What else did they need? Well, yes, something was missing, but they couldn't put a finger on it.

The World Champion Who was "Resurrected"

Life was unfolding in a wonderful way up until the end of the '70s, when Elias faced an opponent so tough that he couldn't overcome him, even though he tried repeatedly. That opponent was the American Wrestling Association (AWA) and the American dollar that it brought when AWA arrived in Australia. The couple who organized and promoted their own wrestling matches, exactly as the rest of the wrestlers did, found it increasingly difficult to compete with the well organized and widely known AWA. Within a few years, Elias's fame began to fade away, and their fortune vanished. A few years later, they had lost everything. Along with their riches, their friends also left them! As the time went by and the family grew without having a steady income, disagreements and quarrels started. Then stress and depression overtook them and shook down their health. That's when Elias decided they should change lifestyles.

The couple bought a twenty-one foot RV. The plan called for touring Australia starting from the North. They'd stop at any town they'd be welcomed at to organize and promote local matches, starting with Golden Beach. Then, they'd move to the next town.

The plan, however, did not work. With nothing accomplished, their stress, depression and disappointment grew heavier. They took an irreversible downturn economically, socially and physically. Their life seemed to have no meaning. The TV was the only thing in which Maureen found consolation and relief.

While flipping through channels late one night, Maureen stopped on a channel were a Salvation Army official was preaching about the need of man to secure a place in the

From Myth to Belief

Kingdom of God now!

"Well, what's *he* talking about?" Maureen thought. "Aren't I a good Christian? Don't I go to church once a month? Don't I even pray occasionally? What am I? A heathen?"

As she continued listening to his preaching, the reading from the Gospel and the words of God, however, she realized that, indeed, she was not as good a Christian as she had thought. She understood that all she knew about God was simply head knowledge and traditional skin-deep religion, a totally non-conscious experience and philosophy. Soon God's spirit brought a heavy conviction on her. She started crying silently. Tears of repentance and sorrow streamed down her cheeks. She had left Jesus out of her life as he waited patiently for so many years. She realized that she had tried to make it on her own and had failed badly. The presence of God became even more intense and overwhelming, overtaking her in this limited space. Even though she could not see Him, she knew He was there. Feeling worthless in front of him, she knelt, worshipped him in his wonderful holy presence, thanked him for loving even her and dedicated her life to him.

When Maureen stood up, she was another person. She had made up her mind. She had made the decision of her life, to change radically. Because she was burning to learn more about God and the savior Jesus, she decided to find the Salvation Army. There they gave her a Bible and helped her in her quest for change. Maureen's life began to improve right away. Stress and depression vanished. She became the supporting pillar of the family.

The World Champion Who was "Resurrected"

Strangely enough, however, her change seemed to split the family. The family had never been involved in God's business before. Seeing their mother's change for the better, her two daughters followed in dedicating their lives to Jesus. Her son resisted strongly, as he did not want to swallow "the bitter pill," as he called religion. Elias was very disappointed because he said he was a "good Christian according to the Greek Orthodox traditional upbringing." As a matter of fact, from the discussions in the family, Elias always thought of Jesus as a deity among the multitude of deities in history. For him, Jesus was like any god or prophet of mankind. They were all deities worthy of worship, and all the people of the world had the right to worship any of them the way they chose. So the Christians worshipped Jesus. This was the only time that Elias had needed to express his beliefs. In fact, he was disappointed because his wife all of sudden gave priority to religious things, forgetting her obligations for work and the survival of the family. Elias had never read the Bible and he did not know that "God does not share His glory with anyone" (Isaiah 48:11). Nor did he know that Jesus, though he existed before the beginning, was born a human from a virgin mother, died, was resurrected, and opened the way to heaven for all men who accept his atonement. He did not know that Jesus is on the right hand of Father God mediating for all people. So, the only thing that Maureen and her daughters could do was to pray for the men of the family.

Wanting to learn more about God, Maureen enrolled and successfully finished a Bible School. During this time, she studied the Word of God and prayed daily, preparing

From Myth to Belief

herself for the work God had for her and her husband. She was sure of it. She could see herself and her husband working together like old times in the wrestling ring, but this time working for the Lord among the Greeks. She couldn't understand how this was possible since Elias was not only in disagreement, he was indifferent as well. After a while, the son decided to allow God to enter his life. He did it with such earnestness that he soon became a leading figure in the church he attended, using the natural talents of leadership and music that God had given him. Meanwhile Elias and Maureen started a wrestling school. Young people enrolled, a dozen at a time. Naturally Elias taught them. All these had a positive effect on the family.

A few years later, the family heard about the Greeks for Christ Ministry. Maureen's heart skipped a beat. "Could it be? But what about Elias?" Then the whole family agonized in prayer on behalf of Elias. The wrestling champion had reached retirement age, and it was then that he opened his heart to the Lord Jesus, as He has the right time for everyone.

All of a sudden, Jesus was not just one of the many world deities for Elias. He became his personal savior, a fact that Elias never missed an opportunity to declare publicly. Thus, as their children started their own married lives, Elias and Maureen became the representatives of Greeks for Christ in Australia, New Zealand and later in Greece.

An old man but still strong and brawny, Elias returned to Greece, the place he had started many years before. He spoke of the love of God to everyone he met. Many who thought him long dead because of his absence from

The World Champion Who was "Resurrected"

Greece's athletic life were surprised to see him standing in front of them. They made the sign of the cross and asked him for an autograph. As Elias signed, he assured them in his fine proverbial humor, "I was really dead until Jesus found me and resurrected me!" Then he shared with them the good news of God's salvation, offered to men through Jesus, which is offered to them personally and freely the same way it was offered to him, a former world heavyweight wrestling champion.

Melbourne, Australia; Greece
As I heard the story from Elias & Maureen Panagos

Now You're a Christian!

You are a Christian by choice, not by birth!

I brought our firstborn son home after his christening, and as I put him in his crib, I said, "Now, my baby, you're a Christian!"

"No, Tina. He's not," I heard a firm voice behind me say. I turned, surprised, but did not see anyone.

"Get behind me, Satan," I muttered.

Soon after that, we moved away from the city of Saskatchewan, Canada, where the beautiful Greek Orthodox Church stands, to the town of Lloydminster, a small town of about 6,000 residents. Not only is there no Greek church in Lloydminister, but there is not another Greek soul to be found!

Over the next five years, I had two more children. We took each one to the Orthodox Church in the big city for the christening and we returned to our little town. Once we entered our home, I would put the baby in the crib and repeat with reassurance the same phrase,

"Now, my baby, you're a Christian!" But every time, I heard the same firm voice behind me.

All three of my children were growing up without Sunday School and church, a fact that I could not bear. I wondered to myself, "How these kids will ever learn about God, as I learned when I was little? Who will teach them the things of God? What do I know to teach them?"

Now You're A Christian!

One day I knelt and prayed these exact words to God aloud. Within two days, a brochure from a neighborhood church showed up at our house.

"If you have children under 13 years old and want to send them to Sunday School, we can pick them up every Sunday morning for Sunday School and drop them off back home later."

Immediately I called and arranged to send our children to Sunday School. Indeed, a polite elderly couple arrived at our home on Sunday morning, introduced themselves, took the children to Sunday School and brought them back.

I was very happy that God heard my prayer. After a few weeks, I began to think that I should go to church someday too. The problem, however, was that the Orthodox churches in Greece and Canada that I attended had made us believe that if we ever went to some other church, the building would fall upon our heads, terrible and awful things would happen to us, etc., so I was afraid to take the risk. On the other hand I thought that if I never went, people would think that my children were orphans! At last I decided to go.

It was a simple and plain Canadian church. I walked in cautiously, somewhat scared. I slowly sat in the very back row somewhere near the door in case something happened. I looked around the congregation. Nobody paid attention to me. I examined the walls, even looked at the ceiling, probably looking like a tourist curiously examining the tall pillars of the Parthenon. I concluded that the building was well built and sturdy, and it seemed to me that it was not about to fall on my head. I heard the preacher talking about the Father, the Son and the Holy Spirit, just like the

From Myth to Belief

preacher did in my own Orthodox church. Since none of the things that I feared were happening, I calmed down a bit, relaxed in my seat. "Hmmm ... it feels good here," I thought. I sat back a little more comfortably.

Meanwhile, my husband's brother and his wife moved to Lloydminster. My sister-in-law found out that I attended a Canadian church once in a while, and one day as we sat in our living room she asked me quite innocently,

"Have you accepted Christ into your heart?"

"What are you talking about?" I shot back. "Don't you see Jesus over there in the family icon shrine and in so many icons all over the house? Haven't I kissed and done the sign of the cross over these same icons at the Greek church that show him by himself or in the arms of the Holy Mother Mary hundreds upon hundreds of times?"

"Great, you do very well," continued my sister-in-law calmly. "But I ask you whether He is also in your heart, whether he's the Lord of your life just like the Bible says, the Bible you believe in... Don't you believe in the Bible?"

"Well — yes — of course, I believe in the Bible. I'm a Christian. What do you think I am? A heathen? But what do you mean 'whether He is in my heart?'"

She took from her handbag a small book with a gold cross on the cover.

"What's that?" I asked.

"A Bible," she answered. "Don't you have a Bible?"

"Do I have a Bible?" I responded sadly. "Not only do I not have a Bible, but I'm twenty-seven years old and I have never even seen a Bible."

"But you said that you're a Christian," my sister-in-law wondered aloud. And shaking her head she added, "How

Now You're A Christian!

you say you're a Christian and have never read, or ever even seen a Bible, which you say you believe in?"

"Hey, they baptized me a Christian! And I spent all my childhood in church and Sunday school. Nobody, nobody either at home or in church or in Sunday school or at school, ever showed me one. They never talked to me about the Bible or told me that it is for me and I should read it," I replied with disappointment.

"Here, look," said my sister-in-law, and she read me John 3:16: "God so loved the world that he gave his one and only Son, that whoever believes in him shall not perish but have eternal life." Then she read some more verses. She explained that I could be born again, spiritually speaking, when I received Jesus in my heart, which meant that I consciously allowed Him to be the Lord of my life. She went on to say that I would then find the happiness and meaning I always searched for when Jesus became my first love and main purpose in my life, as the Bible says.

"Why don't I know all these things? I'm a grown up now, and since I was a little girl I spent my life in church..." I wondered out loud as I reminisced about life in my village of Kastri in Kynouria, Greece where I was born and raised in.

My parents were very God-fearing people, although my father, Yannakis Liberis, was a communist ideologue. After World War II, he was sent to Makronnisos, the barren island-prison for communists. For five years my mother and my grandmother toiled, knitting and sewing to raise three young children. They took us to Sunday school and church consistently, however, and we learned almost all the stories of the church, the Holy Tradition and liturgies

From Myth to Belief

by heart. Most of my uncles on my father's side were well educated individuals, doctors, lawyers, etc. and one of them, Vassilis Liberis, served as Minister of Education to the Greek government.

The most famous man in Kastri, however, was my father, a very well educated man who had studied the encyclopedia inside-out. Since he was also good at working with his hands, he chose to be a blacksmith and entrepreneur. He made farming tools and sold them to farmers. During the week, however, along with the other tools, he made a separate one with extra care, a different one each week, which he took to the Sunday market and gave it away to whoever he thought was most in need. He did this every week on Sunday. So not only was he the most famous man in Kastri, he was also the most well liked. Even now, some twenty years after his death, the children of the village know about him and mention his name with reverence. On the other side of the village another family lived, that of my husband, who will now share his story.

My mother was a saint. My father, however, was brutal and abusive. He swore and beat my mother and us kids violently, and he'd pick a fight with the first man he met. I, the eldest son, who am the spitting image of my mother, I was beat all the more next to my mother. That led me also to become brutal and rude, to be the most rebellious kid around, the one who did all the bad things in the village. Everyone feared me and avoided me like the village's villain boy. When I was eleven or twelve years old, my father suddenly left for Brazil, not so much to work, but rather to run away from his family! Suddenly a heavy burden was lifted off my shoulders and that of our family's.

Now You're A Christian!

I had just finished elementary school. I mustered all the courage I could find and visited the village tailor to ask him for a job. He looked at me in disbelief, and even though he and his wife had their reservations due to my reputation, he took me as his assistant.

Uncle Nick proved to become my father, because apart from the art of sewing, he also taught me how to behave, how to look after the family now that I was its "protector" etc. I started to change, to become a good and useful kid, and I liked it. I had worked for Uncle Nick for three years when I received an invitation to emigrate to Canada. It was from my father who had been invited by a brother who lived there. I arrived in Saskatchewan, Canada, and began work at my uncle's restaurant immediately. All my siblings followed me one by one, each invited by my father.

When I turned twenty-two, my father went to Greece. He found Yannakis Liberis and arranged my engagement to his daughter, Matina. The engagement took place in our village. It was attended by everyone in the village except me! The only reason Matina agreed to marry me was because she did not want to hurt her father whom she loved very much, although her father said his daughter had the last word in her future. Forty days after Matina arrived at Saskatchewan, we had a first class Greek Orthodox wedding. My father's wish when he gave me the congratulatory hand shake at the church was, "Don't let her be the boss!" Soon, Tina was pregnant with our first son, and over the next five years, she gave birth to our second son and our only daughter.

Business was doing great. Tina and I worked harder and harder at our own restaurant we had opened in

From Myth to Belief

Lloydminster. Our family seemed to be a loving, traditional Greek family. That's what outsiders saw. In reality, however, "loving" was the one thing it was not. Tina looked at me from on high, because she came from a good, noble family of the highly educated society, doctors, lawyers and ministers of the government. My family was not of good reputation, and according to my father's wish at our wedding, I was the man of the house, the boss, which I never failed to hold over her head. Our wedding was not based on love or even affection. It was simply an arrangement. When my wife said "white," I said "black."

Really, there was no common ground at all between us. We disagreed on everything and often felt like killing each other. No, I never hit her, nor did she throw any dishes or glasses at me. But there was so much discord, hatred and yelling between us all the time. The only reason we did not part was that Tina respected her father and family so very much that she did not want to burden them with the stigma of a divorce! This suited me fine, because my wife helped me out at work and also raised our children. We therefore settled on this way of life, like many couples of our day and age. This happened for the first nine years of our married life. And now, we arrive at the time in life that my wife had her spiritual pursuits for herself and the children. I was too busy for such things, so I'll have Tina continue our story.

My sister-in-law and I arranged for us to go to another, nearby church. "Since I committed the sin of going to a non-Orthodox church already," I thought "Let me go now to this new one." As soon as we walked in, we found ourselves in a joyful atmosphere. The parishioners were

Now You're A Christian!

happy and smiling. Immediately they hurried to introduce themselves and to welcome us with a big hug.

"It's wonderful here!" I marveled pleasantly. "I've never experienced anything like this in any church I've ever attended. This is what I've been longing for. I really like it here." The singing was heavenly, the prayer touched me, the sermon spoke to my heart, as if God was sitting beside me and speaking only to me. I had been searching exactly for this all my life because I needed it, and I found it at last! At the end of the sermon, the preacher invited people in need of prayer to get up and go to the front of the hall. I ran down, stood alone in front of the pulpit, lifted my hands up to heaven without anyone telling me what to do or say and I prayed to God a prayer that came from deep within me. No one asked me to repeat a certain prayer, no one prayed for me, no one was around me. It was me and God. Actually I did not realize what I was doing. This prayer was flowing out my mouth from deep within me like a torrent. Later I read in the Bible that it is the Holy Spirit who helps the believer pray in times like these. I was praying to the Father, asking him to forgive me and telling him that I loved Him and that I wanted to belong to Him.

I was in a spiritual ecstasy, I would say, when a force from above blew as a fiery wind and threw me down on the floor. No human hand had touched me. No, I was not hurt. It was like the mighty One took me into his supernatural arms and placed me gently on the floor, which felt as though it was made of cotton. At the same time, power flooded my inside and made me feel a very warm feeling of immense love and jubilation, not only permeating my body from head to toes, but staying inside. I don't know

From Myth to Belief

how long I stayed like this, but when I got up I was another person. It was like I floated. Nobody, however, approached me to explain what had happened to me.

On the way home with the kids, I drove by the restaurant. Moments like these in life remain indelibly etched in our memory forever. I walked through the kitchen door in the back, and found my husband standing in front of the oven. He turned his eyes for a moment to see who came in, and he seemed to me like a lucent prince upon his white horse! My heart was filled with an immense love for him. At that very moment I loved him truly for the first time. It was like I was seeing him for the first time and I was falling in love with him at first sight, as the saying goes. I do not know what he saw on me. A halo on my head? A dove on my shoulder? I don't know what, but surprised he asked,

"Hey — what happened to you?"

"I don't know, darling, but I'm very happy," I answered smiling, and I fell in his arms. The same immense and deep love that had flooded my heart at the church for God flooded my heart also here at the restaurant for my husband. I told him nothing, but from that moment on I was no longer the same Tina that Spiro and I knew. My husband always says that from that moment on, an unending sweetness came out of me, from my mouth and my entire being. He had never seen me like this before glowing with love and joy, so loving. Even at night when he came home from work he said,

"Something happened to you, something happened...."
But again, I didn't tell him anything.

A few days later, my sister-in-law again asked me Apostle Paul's scriptural question, "Have you received the

Now You're A Christian!

Holy Spirit since you believed?"

"What's that?" I asked. And immediately I added, "Is it in the Bible?" From my previous experience, I wanted to know only the things that were in the Bible and nothing else. She opened the Bible and read the passages in the Acts of the Apostles, chapter 8, when Peter and John visited the believers in Samaria, and chapter 19 when Paul visited the believers in Ephesus; they encouraged the believers to ask to receive the Holy Spirit.

"If the Bible says so, then it is for me too. I want it," I said with confidence. And I began to pray. Only a few days passed after fervently asking Father God when He gave the Holy Ghost to me, just like he did to the first century Christians whom "The Holy Spirit came on them, and they spoke in tongues and prophesied" (Acts 19:6). The same experience happened to me. This was another great experience that has kept my spirit alive and has filled me with power to witness the name of Jesus Christ to everyone at every opportunity without being ashamed. And now Spiro will continue our story.

A few days later, the preacher of that church paid us a visit. He read the Bible and explained what had happened to Tina. I sat on the edge of the couch and listened silently. When he finished and was ready to leave, he addressed me and said kindly, "You are invited to come to church too, Spiro."

"I'm Greek Orthodox," I said, cutting him off abruptly. As soon as I heard myself, it was like a sharp knife of conviction tore into my heart. "What kind of a Christian am I when I do not know what the Bible says?" I thought "Let alone that I do not even set foot in my church..." But

From Myth to Belief

I replied to the preacher, "I will not prevent my wife from going, however," and I have no idea why I said that. Was it an attempt to drown that conviction? Was it an attempt to avoid the preacher? Was it because I had seen a real change in Tina and I liked it? I don't know. The preacher smiled politely, bid us goodbye, and left.

Every Sunday morning and evening, and every Tuesday evening, Tina would dress the children up. She also got ready herself and all together, they went to church. I kept working hard in our restaurant, but there was a burden on me. Since Tina had had that experience in the church which she had not shared with me, she had stopped lecturing me, as she used to do before. Nor did she tell me to change my ways and my life, or to go with her to church or to accept Christ and so on and on. And this was even heavier on me than her yelling. It was impossible for me to bear. I did not know what had happened or what was going on, but whatever it was, I liked it, and the conviction was growing heavier upon me.

Life went on like this for a while. One Sunday afternoon I got up after my usual Sunday afternoon nap, put on my best suit without knowing why, and I went to work. Puzzled, my wife saw me going to work wearing my best suit instead of the work clothes that I always wore when I went to the restaurant, but said nothing. In the evening she got prepared like every Sunday, took the children, and went to church. This time, however, she stopped by the restaurant. As soon as I saw our car through the wall glass windows, I got my jacket, walked out, opened the car door and sat silently next to her. We arrived and entered the church without having exchanged a word. It was as if

Now You're A Christian!

someone had planned all this, and we silently participated in it. At the end of the service I stood, went to the front of the hall, as my wife had done about a month before, I knelt and crossed my hands so hard that I felt like they had had stuck together, and I prayed the same prayer over and over like the tax-collector, a story that I did not know at the time.

"God, have mercy on me, a sinner. God, have mercy on me, a sinner..."

And even harder, I pressed my hands together until they trembled. I tried to save myself from something I did not know by my own strength. I thought that the more I tried, the easier I could be saved from my sins, as if man's salvation comes from the sincere and hard work of the man. Wasn't that the way I was taught? Wasn't that why I had seen the village women and men crawl on their knees to church, and many others climb dozens of stairs to church, punishing themselves with various sufferings in order to save their souls? So I kept trying, fighting and sweating in order to save myself as I knelt, until someone knelt beside me, put his arm over my shoulder and prayed with me. He said,

"Lord Jesus, help this man, save him, bless my brother." It was as if some power was coming out of that hand, his hand, which softened me. These words of prayer calmed me down progressively and I became like an ice cube slowly melting over fire. I did not understand what happened, but suddenly I became aware of my sins and that I faced God, and that whatever I did by my own strength was not enough to save me. Only then I felt the true meaning of my prayer, "God, have mercy on me, the

From Myth to Belief

sinner." So I surrendered myself into the hands of God. And only then did I feel forgiven, satisfied and really happy. When we left the church, the burden I was carrying was gone. It's wonderful that when you go to church, you really lay your burdens down at the feet of Christ! Besides, what kind of church is it which does not help you do exactly that?

My wife now will share about the changes that have taken place in our home since then, and I will continue later with the intervention of God in our business.

We bought a Bible and began reading it daily. We attended church regularly. Our lives changed dramatically. There were no quarrels, no shouting and yelling or atrocities in our family. I no longer saw my husband from "on high," and he no longer bossed me around. We started to respect each other and to speak politely to each other and to our children, to talk about the problems we encountered rather than trying to solve them with fights. We began to study together the Word of God and to gather around our children for prayer. Even our lives as a couple got the fire that it deserves, the fire that should have existed from the very beginning. Now we're really in love. Joy and happiness began to enter our home. Of course, we faced problems, but they have increased our faith in God and caused us to grow spiritually, as my husband will now share.

One of them, the most important I'd say, had to do with our business. It started as a snowflake and became an avalanche that came close to burying us for two reasons. First, because I did not give proper attention to God's leading, then because I did not consult with my wife about what we should be doing together, even in business. As

Now You're A Christian!

we said before, our restaurant was doing great. We now had two other partners, my brother and my cousin. When a business grows, it sometimes needs more space, so we decided to open a new and much larger restaurant. A little voice inside me, however, kept telling me, "Spiro, you just stay put."

"Yeah, but they'll get this gorgeous, big restaurant, and I'll get stuck in this little ol' hole. My prestige will be ruined. And besides, how would they manage without me? They'll go under without me," I replied to the little voice repeatedly till it was gradually buried.

Without saying anything to my wife, all three of us mortgaged our homes, signed a hefty loan from the bank and quickly built the restaurant. We built a really wonderful, shining, huge restaurant, just the way we dreamed of it. The location of the new restaurant did not have any traffic, however, an "insignificant detail" that we did not even consider. We only saw and admired the beautiful restaurant. We were indifferent to the fact that there was not even a living soul around. Not only that, but we considered ourselves the big shots of the city and thought that we would become a monopoly in town. Everything was bright and shining with we three associates dressed in tuxedos like we were going to the opera, ready to welcome our distinguished customers, except there were none coming. Of course, we were getting two or three customers here and there in the beginning, and the restaurant somehow started going. We three associates immediately put our feet on our grand desks, crossed the arms over our bellies like big lazy businessmen and left our customers to serve themselves. Suddenly there were many bosses and no

From Myth to Belief

workers. Soon our few customers left, but another one, a very, very important one, came looking for us.

It was the bank. The bank that took the restaurant away, along with the houses of my brother and myself, because in the meantime our cousin, smart guy, understood what was happening and jumped off the train of disaster shortly before it derailed.

From being successful in business we suddenly found ourselves unemployed and without a home. We rented our own home from the bank to keep from being homeless! And then I could not find work. Restaurateurs were looking for young assistant cooks so they would pay them basic salary. They did not need expert chefs like me. So I kept returning home discouraged.

I began withdrawing from my own children because I could not feed them. They looked at me as I babysat while my wife worked in a nursing home, and all I saw in their innocent eyes was that I was worthless! That I was not worthy to be their father! That it would be better if I had not brought them to this world! Such crazy thoughts crossed my mind, even the idea of suicide. I felt like I was a big failure in life. Many times, we make the mess ourselves and then we conveniently blame the devil. That's what I did in the beginning. But then that little voice which had told me to stay put came to mind. I then realized that my selfishness prevented me from hearing that little voice as the actual voice of God trying to protect me. I also realized that I had not discussed a very important issue with my wife as I should have. A wrong decision of mine caused my family practically to be thrown in the streets. Fortunately, though, I continued going to church and prayed with my

Now You're A Christian!

wife, which encouraged me to ask God for an impasse. I prayed,

"Give me, my God, a job and I'll work fourteen, even sixteen hours a day. I beg of you!"

Just like the beginning of every month, heavy steps led me to the Bank to pay the rent on May 1st, the rent which we had struggled to scrape up after so much hard effort. As soon as I entered the bank, Pete, the bank manager called me to his office. "Uh oh," I thought. "What now? Will they actually throw us out?"

I entered his office ready to collapse.

"Hi, Spiro. Wonderful day today, eh?" the manager greeted me. Then without waiting for an answer, he asks, "Do you want to buy a restaurant?"

Surprised, I asked, "With what? With buttons?" He laughed.

"Why, of course not! Now don't worry about money. I just want to know whether you want to buy a restaurant. You see that one over there?" he asked me while showing me a little café, just a hole in the wall, across the street from the bank. "They're asking $30,000." I saw he was serious, I assured him that I would speak with my wife (I'd learned this lesson too), and that I'd come back in a few days.

Tina and I went to visit the "restaurant" for coffee. Coffee was all we could afford! As a matter of fact, they didn't have much more than coffee to offer anyway. Although the little restaurant was dead, we liked it. I went back to the bank manager, "I'm offering $15,000," I said. Immediately he got the seller on the phone, turned around and said,

"The seller will accept $20,000." I thought to myself,

From Myth to Belief

"What's another five grand when I'm broke?"

"Agreed," I said. "Agreed," said the seller. The manager hung up the phone, turned around and handed me all the money plus $2,000 to buy a few necessities, all from his own pocket. No bank money was involved because the bank wouldn't lend me a cent with the state of credit I was in.

"But, but ..." I spluttered. "Don't worry," the bank manager assured me quietly. "If you do well, we'll talk again in a year."

I walked out the Bank with $22,000 in my pocket, no contract, no required collateral (which of course I didn't have anyway), nothing binding except my word and a handshake! Do such miracles happen in our time? Yes, because we had prayed to God with all our heart. I learned yet another important lesson that May 1st, 1982. Tina and I and a waitress started work immediately. Along with the restaurant we also started a catering service called SonLight Catering. Business went well, and in one year we doubled the space. Very pleased, the bank manager watched our progress from across the street. In a few months he called me back in his office and asked,

"Do you want to buy the house you now rent?"

"I'd love to," I replied, "but I have yet to put enough money aside for the down-payment."

"Don't worry about it," he assured me. "From now on the bank will put the monthly rent money in a special account so it will get capitalized little by little until you reach the required amount for the down-payment. If you skip even a single payment, however, you will lose this capital."

'But such things don't just happen,' I thought. 'Well,

Now You're A Christian!

maybe this man here is not really Mr. Pete. He just may be St. Peter!'

Indeed we kept paying our monthly payments regularly until we reached the amount of the down payment, and then we bought the house. Although we bought our own house twice, we consider this as yet another miracle in our lives. We sold the restaurant in just seven short years, and with the profit we started another one, a small restaurant in a mall.

About this time, we heard about *Greeks for Christ*, a ministry in Oakland, California, that had spread throughout America, and Canada, and we decided to pay them a visit. When we arrived in Oakland, we were surprised to find that this ministry hosted various other activities such as a Greek radio show on a good number of stations in the U.S. and Canada, publication of videos, magazines and pamphlets, prison ministry, homeless and drug addiction ministry, Bible school, camps, conventions, etc. Before returning to Canada, my wife and I prayed to the Lord to lead us to support Greeks for Christ, because this ministry expresses us perfectly. The problem was that we had no money! So we decided to take a small step of faith. Our family offered the ministry our support in prayer, but also in finances if they agreed to broadcast *The Greek Hour of Hope* radio program in our area too so we and other Greeks in Canada hear it every week. They agreed. We returned home and finished up our twenty-five seat restaurant which we called *Spiro's Steak & Pizza*. Upon opening the store, the phones rang off the hook with orders, and we had to take them off the hook because we couldn't answer them any longer. Customers waited in long lines

From Myth to Belief

to enter. We were forced to expand our restaurant three times to 130-person capacity within several months! Then we realized that our one small step of faith was enough to make the Lord pour out his richest blessings upon us.

Even today, after so many years, God continues to bless us. I sit back and think of where we were and where our Father God has brought us. God forgave and saved us when we prayed, asking him to forgive us from our sins. Due to our unwise actions, we were caught up in debt. We went through difficult times, but we were careful to learn quickly the lessons God wanted us to learn. When we trusted Him completely, taking a step of faith, He not only helped us get gradually out of the difficult position, but he also helped us send all three of our children to good schools and colleges, then get them married to good Christian spouses. Now, we are blessed with grandchildren. We also bought another, much better home. The Lord allows us to continue attending our good and blessed church, to do well in our business, and to become a blessing to others, even to our own family and relatives. What we learned is that God is not a respecter of persons, but he responds to the sincere prayer of any man, making him an over-comer of any problem. My wife will close now with a short but important example of God's love and care, which she experienced during her mother's last days.

I rushed to Greece from Canada and found my mother in the hospital. All night I prayed about how to talk to her so that she would prepare for the big trip to eternity. Suddenly I jumped out of sleep in the middle of the night with three phrases in my mind. "Jesus, forgive me. Jesus, come into my heart. Jesus, take me home." In the morning I

Now You're A Christian!

rushed to the hospital. She immediately recognized me, although she'd started slipping into coma. I was alone with her talking for some time. After a short silent prayer to God to give her and myself grace, I told her,

"Mom, I want you to do me a favor."

"Sure, my daughter," she said.

"I want you to repeat after me."

"Ok."

"Jesus, forgive me," I began.

She looked at me briefly and then repeated, "Jesus, forgive me."

"Jesus, come into my heart," I continued.

Immediately, she repeated, "Jesus, come into my heart," and I could see her face beaming peace already.

"Jesus, take me home," I finished.

"Jesus, take me home," she concluded. She took a deep breath, paused for a moment, and then prayed without my leading. "Jesus, forgive me. Jesus, come into my heart. Jesus, take me home." Her face took an expression of satisfaction and delight. "*NOW* you're a Christian, mom!" I said to myself.

Soon my mother fell into a coma from which she never came out. In two days she was taken home, to Christ's home. Praise the name of the Lord!

Lloydminster, Canada
As I heard the story from Spiro and Tina Kokonas

Stories of Lives Changed

In John 15, Jesus describes his followers as people who "bear fruit" (verse 16), "more fruit" (verse 2), "much fruit" (verses 5 and 8) and "fruit that will remain" (verse 16). Just as the fruit of an apple tree is an apple, the fruit of a follower of Jesus Christ is another follower of Jesus Christ. The following section of this book talks about the fruit of the Greeks for Christ ministry teams and those who have provided the spiritual and material resources for that ministry. In a productive vineyard, many labor doing many different tasks over a long period of time to finally bring about the harvest. So it is in the Kingdom work of which Jesus spoke. "I planted, Apollos watered," wrote the Apostle Paul, "but God was causing the growth" (1Corinthians 3:6).

The fruit Jesus spoke of is eternal fruit. In this analogy Jesus conjures up the image of a grapevine heavily laden with large clusters of juicy grapes. In the preceding chapters of this book you have read the accounts of people whose lives have been touched and changed for eternity. In this final section you will continue reading about "fruit that remains," people whose lives were impacted somewhat indirectly, not unlike a seed in a grape that fell from the harvester's basket, germinated in soil outside the vineyard and took root before it too produced fruit.

Just as the branch is connected with the vine for its nourishment, so Jesus admonished His followers to "abide in Him," to stay connected with Him, reminding them that "without Me you can do nothing." All spiritual fruit is the outcome of our being intimately connected with Christ who is our Vine. As one who has followed the ministry of Greeks for Christ for many years, I have heard passionate and repeated calls for prayer from Dr. Peter Vourliotis. "Pray for the broadcasts; pray for the meetings; pray for the literature; pray for the team members; pray for the church," he pleads. Like a faithful laborer in the vineyard, he has carefully and prayerfully utilized every tool available to tap the divine nutrients by which to touch the hearts of eternal souls.

Only God knows how to truly measure the harvest. He leaves out the wood, hay and straw when making His assessment, as He transforms those clusters of fruit into eternal treasures of gold, silver and precious stones (1 Corinthians 3:12). In the remaining chapters you will read about the gold, silver and precious stones for which the laborers have toiled, the precious Holy Spirit has drawn and our dear Redeemer has washed in His blood to the glory of our Father, the Husbandman of the vineyard.

Andy Lay
Sylmar, South California

Andy Lay has been Executive Director of Development/Senior Director of Development of Fuller Theological Seminary, Pasadena, CA, since 2003, where he completed his graduate studies in Theology. Rev. Lay has pastored churches in Missouri and Tennessee. He has also served as an executive or director of various ministries and Bible colleges and universities, such as the Union Rescue Mission, African Enterprise, Every Home for Christ, World Vision USA, Children's Network International, Christian Management Association, Fresno California Christian College, Benton Harbor Free Will Baptist College, Moore, OK, Every Home for Christ Albania, etc. Andy has three children, six grandchildren and five great-grandchildren and lives with his wife Magdalene in Sylmar, California.

A Lifelong Adventure

*Adventure for the sake of adventure
is simply an experience.
The adventure with Christ, however,
is an exciting way of life.*

In the auditorium of the American school in Cali, Colombia, a small group of our high school students spoke about the calm and protection they felt when they had been in grave danger. During a church retreat in the countryside, a group of armed guerrillas had held them captive, threatening to kidnap them. Yet, these young people felt peace and security throughout the ordeal.

As I listened, I thought of my early high school days in Brooklyn, New York, in the '70s. Though everything had been going well for me, I did not feel the serenity that those young people had, even when terrorists were threatening them with guns. I had been captain of the volleyball team, an editor of the yearbook, a good student, and I had lots of friends. Yet, the normal teenage questions, insecurities and doubts, and the problems around me, kept me from the sense of peace these students described.

I grew up on 81st street in Brooklyn. In the '60s, my life was like one of the old TV sitcoms. All summer, we played hide and seek, climbing across the backyards on the block. During the rest of the year, we attended public school. My family was the only Greek family on the block,

From Myth to Belief

but we attended the Assumption Greek Orthodox Church which kept us close to the Greek faith and traditions. In spite of everything going well, I was scared of life and I was very shy. I did not like to take risks. My comfort zone was very limited and I stayed inside it.

The fact that I did not speak Greek to follow the long liturgy, so I thought, did not prevent me from becoming religious. I learned all the prayers by heart, missed no church services, observed all the fasting days, confessed and attended Sunday school regularly. I was doing my best to be the "best believer" I could. Later I realized that the people who spoke Greek also did not understand the liturgy. I followed it through a translation pamphlet like everyone else.

However, one holiday, as I stood in the crowded aisle of the church next to a long line of icons, a doubt came to me about God. It seemed to me that church and religion were important in society to keep up Greek and other traditions, but was God real? I had tried so hard to practice all the Orthodox rituals, and yet I had not found God; I did not know Him. I started to question Greek Orthodoxy and Christianity and all religions in general. Maybe God and religions were all myths created to give people hope, because we were so alone in the world.

Eventually, I rejected the faith of my fathers along with all religions, and I was defending atheism in my high school classes. My new position was that God was a myth invented by the ruling class in order to keep the masses under control. Furthermore, I believed that educated people should scorn the fairytales about God and realize there is nothing other than humans to keep the world going

A Lifelong Adventure

for good or for bad. This position of mine, however, did not provide me with a secured peace deep in my heart. We were living through Vietnam and the threat of nuclear war, the energy crisis and racism of the sixties. Humans were messing up the world and it was frightening. On the other hand, people talked about peace, and I didn't have it. One of my friends named Lisa, however, seemed always to be quietly happy, secure and full of peace.

Near the end of 11th grade, on a Friday evening, I was with Lisa and a large group of her church friends. At the end of the meeting, she prayed. It shocked me that my friend could just talk to God, in front of a crowd of people. She seemed so sure that God was alive and that He was listening to her. Later, that night, alone in my house, I spoke with God in a way I hadn't before. As a kid, I had said my prayers, repeating the "Lord's Prayer," but that night I just talked. I longed for the calm and assurance that my friend always seemed to have. I didn't know how to obtain these things, but for the first time, I believed that God was alive. I asked Jesus to come into my life and forgive my sins. My life then changed radically and has never been the same since. I started on an adventure led by Jesus that continues until today.

In another year, I was commuting to college. Among the many challenging and exciting opportunities at Barnard College in New York was a Bible study. These college students and recent graduates read the Bible voraciously and shared their insights and discoveries at the meetings. What they read matched the joy and excitement they were experiencing as they served Jesus. Knowledgeable about many places of the world, they often prayed for places I

From Myth to Belief

had not heard of. Their undergraduate and graduate studies had them entering law, finance, and medicine, and they used what they were learning in prayer and expected to serve the Lord in those fields. They spoke of occupying positions for Jesus, serving Him wherever the Lord led them. So I liked the group from the first day I was invited to attend.

While we were praying at one of these meetings in my sophomore year, I sensed the Lord tell me that He would call me to Cali, Colombia. My instinct was to say no. I could not leave my family and city for an unknown place. However, I was scared to say no to God. I told Him I would go where He led, but He had to make His leading very clear. On my way to class, a few weeks later, I saw a poster that said, "Your New York State teaching license is accepted in these countries." The country names formed a curling spiral. When I found Colombia on the list, I joined the Education Program.

Four years later, I had an undergraduate degree in English Literature, a New York State teacher's licenses for high school Social Studies and English, and I was two months away from receiving a Master's degree in History. Some years before, on the IRT subway traveling home from a Bible study, I had been baptized in the Holy Spirit. As graduation from Columbia Graduate School neared, I was ready to start on my adventure. I fasted and prayed to the Lord for guidance. Within a week, I was offered a position that I seemed particularly prepared for, but it was in New York, not in Colombia. I held off accepting the position and continued to seek the Lord. One night at a Bible study, a man of God asked me if I had ever thought

A Lifelong Adventure

of teaching in Colombia. When I told him that I had been praying about it for several years, I was put in touch with the principal of the American School in Bogotá. Soon, I was on a 747 jumbo jet on my way to South America.

I wasn't sure exactly how I would serve the Lord in Colombia, but I tried to take opportunities to witness to His truth and nature. As I taught U.S. History to energetic middle school students, I was always looking for ways to emphasize the Lord's hand in the forming of the nation. During recess, on the basketball court or eating lunch with my students, I tried to be an example of Christ's love and compassion. After school, there were clubs and other activities where I could occupy a place for Jesus. When the non-sectarian school faced harsh situations, like a severe illness or a kidnapping, I might be called on to pray in a school assembly.

On Sundays, I attended Mount Zion, a house church, where all present were expected to minister in the meetings, so that "Speaking the truth in love, we will in all things grow up into him who is the Head, that is, Christ. From him the whole body, joined and held together by every supporting ligament, grows and builds itself up in love, as each part does its work." (Ephesians 4:15-16). Each of us had to be alert to the leading of the Holy Spirit. Themes and teachings came forth week after week from a variety of people who shared what the Lord was teaching them in the Bible, and from their relationship and experience with Him.

In 1989, over 100 bombs exploded in Bogotá. Those days of danger unsettled the Bogotano population, leading them to seek new sources of security. During the weekend,

From Myth to Belief

a group from Mount Zion would go to the main plaza, near the President's mansion downtown. Singing and speaking, we encouraged people to receive the love and peace that the Lord brings when we accept Him as our Savior. Many of us held prayer meetings in our neighborhoods, at the universities, at out places of work. We supported each others' efforts to share the gospel to families, neighbors and friends.

I grew up, spiritually and naturally, in Bogotá. After eight years, having never forgotten the Lord's call to Cali, Clarita, a Colombian believer and I left the capital and headed to the fertile valley of Cali. We preached on the streets, witnessed to colleagues at work, and ministered to the sick. Today, a small group of maturing believers meets in a house where, as in the ancient churches in the Holy Land and Greece, and as at Mount Zion and my home church in NY, we minister to each other as Paul taught the Corinthians, "What then shall we say, brothers? When you come together, everyone has a hymn, or a word of instruction, a revelation, a tongue or an interpretation. All of these must be done for the strengthening of the church." (1 Corinthians 14:26).

Our small church has young people who need mentoring and elderly people who need encouraging, and all of us need to continually walk in the plan the Lord has for us. We preach in parks on Sunday afternoons, invite unsaved friends and family to Christmas gatherings in December and because "we are God's workmanship, created in Christ Jesus," we are always looking for those "good works which God prepared in advance for us to do" (Ephesians 2:10).

A Lifelong Adventure

The Lord has graciously permitted me, who never wanted to leave my city, to travel to many places. One summer, my mother invited me to accompany her to California. We visited the sights of San Francisco and drove along the coast. Looking for a place to worship on Sunday, we found a Yellow Pages listing for a Greek church in Oakland. A Spirit filled Greek church? It was one of the highlights of my life to have worshiped the Lord with many young and old people from Greece and the US, even Yayas (Grandmothers), their black sweatered arms held high in the air as they praised the Lord. Since that time, it has been a blessing to follow the ministry of Greeks for Christ as they witness to Greek-Americans and Greeks on two sides of the Atlantic and beyond and to receive uplifting and encouraging notes from the Ministry.

Back in the 1970s, I started on an adventure that led me from high school, through college and, twenty-four years ago, to Colombia, South America. I have done things I never planned on, in places I never imagined. Most have been very satisfactory and agreeable, like working at schools in Colombia, encouraging refugees from a volcano eruption and mentoring underprivileged kids in Cali. Some have been dangerous. Guerrillas on motorcycles have escorted me into a small town as I drove through the countryside. Bandits stopped and robbed the bus I traveled on over a mountain pass. I witnessed firsthand the attack that destroyed the Palace of Justice just three blocks from my apartment. Through these and in the more usual challenges of life, this timid Brooklyn gal has always felt peace and been protected.

Once, when I was backpacking from Bogotá, Colombia

From Myth to Belief

to Quito, Ecuador, I was unexpectedly asked to speak about my life to a large group of teenagers in Ibarra, Ecuador. I told them I was on an adventure with Jesus. I didn't always know what was next, but it would be exciting. Today, I am still on that adventure, and I trust God to lead me to the next and on every part of my journey in life.

People tend to think of finding God or following God as difficult or boring, maybe something to start considering when they're older. St. Paul described following Jesus as an adventure. We don't always know exactly what's ahead, but God promises that it is better than anything we could have designed or even imagined. What God has planned for us is good, pleasing and perfect. However, if we want God's will for our life, we have to choose His will. It doesn't just happen accidentally or automatically. If we do the will of God, we will never be disappointed. God's will for us fits exactly the person we are becoming in Him. Whether we serve Jesus around our neighborhood or around the world, life is an exciting journey full of peace when guided by God Himself.

Bogota, Cali, Colombia
As I heard the story from Georgia Costalas

One Day All Will be Well...

> *"Delight yourself in the Lord and he will fulfill your desires."*
> *Psalm 37:4*

Imagine an eight year old girl much taller than others her age, slim like a tender reed by the river, wearing orthopedic shoes and having one eye covered with a black patch to correct amblyopia. Not even a pirate's daughter would look like this! Ever since I can remember myself, all children made fun of me. And how could a little girl like me be good for anything? Perhaps only good for mowing the back yard. This is what I did, always crying, until one day even God felt sorry for me. He told me while I was mowing,

"One day all will be well!" From then on, all the fun kids poked at me was like water running off a duck's back.

I was born in the city of Pine Bluff, Arkansas. I was a very shy, introverted child who seemed to carry the burdens of the whole world on my back. At the age of seven I dedicated myself to God. My parents were divorced when I was about twelve years old, and both remarried. I found myself going to London, England, with my Mom and stepdad because he worked in the Air Force. England is where I graduated from high school.

By the age of fourteen, my body had transformed into that of an adult woman, five feet-nine inches tall with

From Myth to Belief

loose blond hair and bright brown eyes that could catch anyone's attention, even across the street. I caught the attention of men from far away. In England, of course, I was still very shy and introverted. In high school I was contemplating what the Lord had told me, that someday all would be well, so I decided to go out of my protective shell and face the world, trying everything, doing things and meeting new people, even if it proved adventurous. So a rapid transformation happened to me. I went from shy to much more outgoing. From day to day, classmates said they could not even recognize me because I was changing so quickly. It was then that I pulled away from God. But it was also then that I met a young and handsome American man who served in the U.S. Air Force. His name was Bill and was from Ohio. He liked me, I liked him too, so we began dating.

Little by little I evolved into the undisputed leader in my class. I always had the leading part in the theatrical plays at school and at church. I became the best softball player in school, and certainly the leader of our team. I also evolved to be the fastest 100-meter runner in school. When my classmates found themselves in a deadlock on any issue, they'd come to me to find solutions. I also took advantage of another natural advantage of mine: my photographic memory.

It seems that I had asked for something over my head when I decided to try anything adventurous, as it happened with the traditional 11-day Senior class trip to the "eternal city," of Rome. Upon arriving at the airport, the immigration authorities delayed me for four hours. "Procedural" they said, and apologized. In these four hours, however, they

One Day All Will be Well...

found out everything about me. Who I was, where I was born, my parents' jobs, even the University of Texas in Dallas that I planned to attend after high school. In the following days, wherever I went I met a tall, handsome, clean shaven thirty-five year old man with straight black hair and shiny black shades. This extra polite gentleman (who even addressed me by my name) or his "people" relentlessly created attractive situations for me and my classmates until he convinced us to let him take us on a city tour in Rome.

When he arrived at the hotel door in the most glittering limousine I have ever seen to pick us up, I realized that his intentions were far from showing us old tourist attractions. After just a few minutes of driving, our limo was joined at a city square by many more black cars that looked like London cabs. Immediately I used my photographic memory to record the license plate numbers in my mind. We then drove for what seemed like hours down a dark, lonely road outside of Rome. It was just us, all the other cars had disappeared. I was awestruck when we arrived at our destination. A crystal mansion built on a huge rock at the edge of the water glittered in front of us. And before I could catch my breath, all those black cars reappeared suddenly and parked on either side of our limo. All of the people I had seen over the past few days, taxi drivers, waiters, tour guides, porters and even the immigration officers who had delayed me, some fifty of them, were present and gazing hungrily at us three American girls. As soon as they took us to the top floor overlooking the water, I took the clean shaven aside, looked him in the eye and said,

From Myth to Belief

"Look. Both the Foreign and the Education Ministries of the United Kingdom and the Scotland Yard are informed ahead of time about school trips out of the country like ours. They have a way of following us and they know exactly where we are every day of our trip. Every license plate number of every vehicle we board is written down by a plain-clothed person just in case something happens to us. For instance, we know the license plate numbers of your limousine and cars. They are..." I recited to him the license plate numbers of his limousine and the other cars parked outside. "So the best thing you can do is to take us back to our hotel, because you'll be in a tough spot when they find us in a little while."

As I was finishing my little speech I, saw his hands trembling slightly. With an effort, however, he took a deep breath and smiled.

"Now, you believe you scared me to death."

Then he cleared his throat, called his lieutenant Luigi over and whispered something in his ear. Luigi gave an order aloud to the rest of the gang members in Italian, they turned around and we all exited the crystal mansion, got back in the limo and cabs and returned to our hotel. Immediately I visited the tourist police. There I learned that the handsome Italian gentleman was called Bruno and he was the most wanted gangster of the most infamous crime syndicate in Rome. The reason he attempted to kidnap me was that I was sixteen year-old, tall, shapely and blonde!

I found the accuracy of what the police told me later in Dallas, Texas, where I learned that a young, tall, blonde and beautiful Texan American exchange student in Rome

One Day All Will be Well...

had been kidnapped. She was kept in a remote villa for two years, and was shackled naked, along with several other girls, as outlets for the sexual appetites of members of a gang, maybe the Mafia. When the girls reached the age of thirty, the gang would kill them. When a gangster carelessly left the chain unlocked, she had the chance to escape naked and run into the streets to ask for help. She eventually returned home to the United States. Such abductions, I learned, happened very often in Italy. I am sure that God protected me in a very special way in this case, even though I was running away from his will.

Once I graduated high school in England, I returned to the U.S. and started attending the University of Texas in Dallas. I lost contact with Bill, of course. Much later I had a date with some young man I met in Dallas. I was getting prepared for the date when there was a knock on the door. I opened the door and, to my big surprise, Bill was standing there. Instead of saying anything else, like "hi," or "how are you," he asks, "Do you want to become my wife?"

I went insane, forgot my appointment, and we go get married that very moment. Immediately after, we moved to Ohio near Bill's family. I got a job as a journalist with the Wheeling News-Register. I believe that the Lord gave me the job, as they had many experienced reporters with degrees and such applying for it. I have a degree, but not in journalism, and I had no experience. At first they told me at the office that they would send an older journalist to show me the ropes of reporting, but they never did. In six months they offered me the position of editor, which I did not accept, simply because I had too much fun being

From Myth to Belief

a reporter. However, they forced me to do the work of the editor when the boss was on a sick leave or on vacation. So as a reporter, I covered all kinds of topics from presidential elections to assorted political events. I covered the inauguration of President Jimmy Carter and I had top privileges in Washington, DC. I also covered natural disasters and accidents, in addition to local news and investigative crime reports.

My problem was that I uncovered too much. In fact, many a time I was "relieved of my duties" when the story was too dangerous, because as my boss liked to say they were "afraid they would find me in the bottom of Ohio River with a block tied around my neck!" I've had police guarding our house and watching over me because of threats on my life. I remember once when I revealed sensitive information about a major drug case, the Chief of Police paid us a visit and announced very seriously to Bill and me that if "one of us happened to die" it would look like a suicide or a horrible accident! He even gave Bill a phone number and a name to contact in Washington, DC, as it would be murder. Plus he provided the drug dealer's name. Of course I refused to let some druggie make me live in fear. I brought the matter to our church. We prayed over it and I went on with my life. Well, perhaps I looked behind my back every once in a while.

After sixteen years of marriage, life flowed conventionally. Although we were in love when we got married, our problems grew so many and strong that I decided to leave Bill. But before the divorce was issued I suggested,

"If you promise me that we can start going to church I

One Day All Will be Well...

will not leave you." He agreed and so we started going to church. There I found the opportunity to re-dedicate my life to Jesus and immediately our son Carson, who was then only fifteen years old, followed suit. In exactly one and a half years, Bill also decided to devote his life to God and the whole family then started a new happy life. It's worth mentioning Bill's conversion.

Bill had smoked since the age of nine and had gotten up to five packs of cigarettes a day. He had tried to quit many times, as he knew smoking was taking a toll on his lungs and health. I was always glad when he lit up again, as he was a bear when he tried to quit. He just could not quit no matter how hard he tried. One night I prayed to the Lord that if Bill didn't yield his life to Him Sunday morning at church, I'd file for a divorce on Monday morning. On Saturday night he went to our neighborhood grocery store to buy cigarettes. Right there in the middle of the grocery aisle, he knelt and asked the Lord to take away the smoking habit. He dropped it and immediately asked the Lord to come into his heart and forgive him. It was instant delivery. No more reaching for the matches, no reaching for a cigarette, no more desire.

Then God spoke to Bill and me separately that we'd be in a traveling ministry and bless thousands. We thought that this would happen immediately, but it was not so.

Life went on as before, each one of us in our own work. I, as a journalist, applied to fly in the Eagle F-15 fighter jet, but the committee denied me. I skipped the committee and addressed it to Jesus, and in two weeks, I was already at Andrews Air Force base in Washington, DC, for training. Then they sent me to continue my training at Langley

From Myth to Belief

Air Force Base in Virginia, so I flew in the back seat of the fighter as a Weapon Systems Operator. We fought tough air battles and did difficult maneuvers for two and a half hours. Following that, I flew in a Phantom F-4 for another two and a half hours doing air-ground maneuvers and dropping live bombs in the desert. Then I flew in the Supersabre F-100, doing air refueling missions, and then some smaller military planes and helicopters. I even flew the Goodyear Blimp twice.

In 1986, NASA announced a "reporter in space" project. I applied immediately and was accepted. Already I dreamed that I was flying it back to earth myself and I was searching my Bible for a passage to read to the world as we entered the Earth's atmosphere. I was looking for the one that reads that I "shall mount up with wings as eagles," (Isaiah 40:31) but God showed me another one that reads "Thou hast ascended on high" (Psalm 68:18). Right then, I understood the meaning of the words He told me years ago when I was little that "one day all will be well!" And then God asked me three times, "Do you trust me?"

"Yes, Lord," I replied each time.

Within three hours the Challenger exploded and the "reporter in space" project was cancelled. From what I know, NASA has not offered this program since. I didn't know if this cancelled out what God had given me. I just knew I felt like I was on standby in my spirit. I realized once again that the timing in God's mind is not what I expect or design it to be.

Meanwhile, Bill had his own job and his own hobby, golf. Indeed Bill is an excellent golfer! When he disappeared, I knew I'd find him on the golf course. I continued the

One Day All Will be Well...

work of the reporter, but I had not forgotten my decision in England to try everything, even if adventurous. I learned skydiving. I started to drive formula cars, and I learned to drive high cc bikes, eighteen-wheeler trucks, tractors, excavators and other earthmoving equipment, including steamrollers, not for living of course, but for the fun of it. Now we have a camper and of course, I drive it!

It was then that we moved to Northern California. My mind went to God's promise that He would use us in His work, but again it was not the God's timing. So both Bill and I were hired by the Standard Oil Company. In the San Francisco Bay Area, I found the opportunity to further my studies and submitted an application to the semi-professional women's San Francisco Warriors basketball team, now known as the Golden State Warriors. They hired only forty out of two hundred young women, and I was selected. We started the athlete's fast track life with travel, television, etc. The only problem was that a professional women's team was too far ahead of its time, so it was soon dissolved. I enjoyed it for as long as it lasted.

Our life in California was beautiful, but we decided to return to Texas. We moved close to my mother in the town of Whitesboro, some seventy-five miles north of Dallas. As soon as we moved, I fell seriously ill. I bled from the mouth, from the lungs to be exact. My mother rushed me to the hospital where after many tests, doctors discovered a large tumor just behind my lungs. The nuclear physician gave me the bad news, adding that there was "no hope," and that "ten out of ten patients die." Immediately, doctors began talking about a serious, long, and unsure surgery during which they would open my chest to remove the

From Myth to Belief

tumor. It would take me a long time to recover, they said. If, however, they found the tumor to have spread to my spine, then they could no longer do anything for me.

Immediately I realized the gravity of my situation, and as soon as the doctors walked out of my room, I asked my Father God for the cup to pass from in front of me in the name of Jesus. God must have given me such great faith, because once I finished my prayer I received a strong assurance in my heart that the surgery would never happen. From that very moment I told every doctor, every nurse, every patient and every visitor, "There will be no surgery." Following that, I visited the surgeon at his office and made him promise me that he would take a final CAT scan before the operation. He did take one right then, and I went home to wait for the results.

Early the next day I arrived at the hospital to get the results with incredible peace in my heart. The nurses, however, grabbed me and began preparing me for surgery. Suddenly the door opened and in walked the surgeon. "Carol, Carol," he exclaimed with enthusiasm. "A miracle has happened inside of you. There's no tumor anymore!" Immediately I jumped out of the room, praising God. I ran back to the hospital rooms telling everyone I met, the doctors, the nurses, the patients, everyone, that God had healed me. Some nurses were in tears. Others emphasized to me that I alone would be responsible for whatever might happen to me if I left the hospital. I assured them with a broad smile that I'd call right away if something went wrong.

I entered the room of a girl who suffered from the same disease as mine. They had just found a tumor behind her

One Day All Will be Well...

lungs.

Her name was Mary. I asked her, "Mary, are you a Christian?"

Very weakly, she replied, "half and half."

I said, "Now, Mary, that's what you put in your coffee! Would you like to know Jesus personally?"

"Yes," she said. Then I prayed with her and led her through the sinner's prayer. At first her voice was so weak that I could hardly hear her. But the more we prayed, the stronger it became, growing very bold and with confidence. The next morning, my Mom and I went back to the hospital to visit Mary. As soon as we arrived they informed us she had just passed away! Immediately I glorified God. Even if my illness was meant just to lead Mary to Christ, it was worth it. I cannot always understand God's plans and I don't have answers for everything, but I know I believe in a God whom I can trust completely. And everyone can.

This experience, along with Bill and I losing our jobs almost simultaneously, not because of our fault, marked the beginning of our ministry to God. We had not forgotten God's promise that we would serve Him. We just waited for the moment when He would send us to His work. I was praying with this in mind when Bill decided to go on the Senior Pro Golf Tour. He even had a sponsor. Bill was a scratch golfer and going full-time into golfing would allow him eight to ten hours a day to get practice and get even better. I got excited and even wanted to be his caddy, but I went on praying too. I said in my prayer, "My God, if now is the time to get busy in your work, then, let Bill's golfing go bad." The next day out on the course, Bill could not hit the ball. He double-hit it in one swing. The ball

From Myth to Belief

hooked severely, the ball sliced severely, the ball went even behind Bill's head on one of the swings. He was extremely frustrated and made an audible announcement that he had never golfed that horribly in all his life. Then he noticed that I was dying laughing. I confessed my prayer. Right there we just packed up and went home. We both knew that the time to serve God had just arrived.

We organized rallies in California for only two weeks, but congregations were so blessed that they asked us for more, so we stayed for another six weeks. We returned home for a while and off we went again for another seven weeks. This has gone on for eighteen years now! It was good to have worked in conventional jobs previously, but it is far better now that we are working in the fields of God. We have plowed across America, preaching the gospel of Christ to countless souls. We have seen the hand of God powerfully all the years of our service. And the Lord has never left or abandoned us.

In one of our first trips to California we visited the Greek Church in Oakland. Immediately we bonded with the believers and the work they do for the Lord, because our ministries looked so much alike. Just like us, *Greeks for Christ* preached the simple gospel of Christ not only in America, but wherever Greeks are located. They use a radio network program and online streaming that covers the whole world. They publish music, video, printed and digital material and they work tirelessly and by all means available to tell Greeks and non-Greeks that there is also another way to solve their problems, another way to make themselves and their families happy, an alternative kind of life of different values: those of Christ's. We love the

One Day All Will be Well...

Greeks for Christ ministry, following their work with interest, praying to the Lord for them and visiting them often as we carry the same burden in our hearts for our fellow sinners.

We have been perfectly happy now that we are at the center of God's will. Our whole family is happy. Our son Carson and his wife Val are firm believers, serving the Lord in California.

Our twenty-two year old grandson and his wife, who live with their six month old daughter in Oklahoma, also have a promise from God that they will serve Him too. Our other twenty-two year old grandson, who attends the University of California at Berkeley, loves Jesus with all his heart. Even our year old great-granddaughter yells with delight, "Jesus loves me!"

I look back on my life and see that God has never left me. Even when I was distant from him, he did not leave me unprotected. And yet, I remember myself crying when I was little, when God promised me that everything would be fine with me some day. The promise is not only perfectly fulfilled in my life, but it has exceeded even my wildest expectations. Glory to His name!

Whitesboro, Texas
As I heard the story from Carol Bartolomucci

How Often Do You Read the Bible?

> *"All Scripture is given by inspiration of God, and is profitable for doctrine, for reproof, for correction, for instruction in righteousness."*
> 2 Timothy 3:16

"When I decide to have an unpleasant day, a day empty of love, joy, patience, affection, all that fills the heart with joy, the radiant face of God in my life, then, I do not read the Bible that day."

This is my standard reply when people ask me why I read the Bible every day. In a world that prefers to stumble in the suspect dark alleys of immorality rather than to walk the straight path of morality, that prefers to choose whatever lifestyle seems appealing to them instead of the right one, that has painted all the values of life in grey, we will someday reap the corresponding rotten fruit of our behavior unless we turn to the Bible in time for early education and instruction from God.

I was nineteen years old when I was inspired to start reading the Bible every day by a strange dream. I saw a peer of mine of the same age who was killed in a car accident two years before. She wore no makeup, and she was pale, sad and silent. I asked her, "Why don't you come to dances anymore?" There was no answer. And again,

How Often Do You Read the Bible?

"Why are you so sad? Why are you not wearing makeup?" But again there was no answer. She simply looked at me with the same sad look. Then suddenly I remembered that she had died. "Wait a minute, you're dead," I said. "I remember I saw your picture in the newspaper. I even read the accompanying obituary. How come you're just standing in front of me alive?" I was so upset that I lost my grip on my handbag, and it disappeared somewhere. When I realized that I had lost it, I started looking for it, forgetting the girl. When I finally found it, I opened it immediately to see if someone had stolen my wallet. But instead of money or anything else that I usually carried, I found a small New Testament. I turned my eyes to the girl like I was lost, but she was not there anymore.

The first thing I did in the morning when I got up was to open my desk drawer. There I found the same New Testament, which I had bought six months before, but had left it untouched and forgotten in a drawer. I took it in my hands and started examining it all around the outside first. Then I opened it to the beginning, and within the first three pages, I found a calendar/program for reading the entire New Testament in a year by studying a little bit of it every day. "What important things could this little booklet tell me that I would have to read it every day?" I wondered.

In New York where I lived the first twelve years of my life, my parents took me to the Orthodox Church. They put me in the choir when I was nine or ten, and I remember we chanted "Kyrie Eleison" and "Amen" in unison when the conductor raised his hand. I did not attend Sunday School, however, because the church did not have one. I started Sunday School at twelve when we moved to Philadelphia.

From Myth to Belief

I was very confused when the teacher spoke of God and Christ separately, and only much later on did I realize that the poor little baby of Christmas, the teacher who "taught the common things in a new way and the new things in a common way," the healer of the sick, the Risen Christ of Easter, He is the Lord of Lords and King of Kings, He himself God the Son, the One who could be my friend, brother, teacher, savior and Lord.

I started by reading the verses for each day, Hebrews chapter 12, verses 1 and 2. "Let us run with endurance the race that is set before us, looking unto Jesus, the author and finisher of our faith." And in chapter 10, verse 36, "You have need of endurance, so that after you have done the will of God, you may receive the promise." I, who was always so very anxious, opened my eyes wide. I was under the impression the runner runs as fast as he can to win the race. But here the author talked about the struggle of life and gave specific instructions on how to earn it, the instructions being "looking unto Jesus." There was a gap that was growing inside of me as I was growing up that nothing could fill, a gap caused by the confusion of thoughts and ideas, by the feeling of oppression, by my queries about everything in life, by the uncertainty of everything around me. My big question, "What is life about anyways?" was hanging like a sword over my head. For all of these things, I discovered that there were answers in the New Testament when I started reading it regularly and systematically.

As a matter of fact, whenever I encountered the word "you" or any passage in the second person, I took it personally, like God was speaking exclusively to me.

How Often Do You Read the Bible?

Many times I cried as I felt his truth, his love, his sacrifice, his interest in me. In the Gospel of John, chapter 3, verse 3, I read something that shook me by my foundations, "If you're not born again, you will not see the kingdom of God." And I decided to ask the Lord Jesus Christ to "give birth to me," that I would be born again in a spiritual sense. Suddenly, all of my questions found answers. Life in itself changed for me. The study of the Word of God and prayer have resulted in finding instruction in my life. I am being continually renewed as I walk victoriously and with purpose.

Immediately I started looking for other Christians, for people studying the Bible. I regret to say that I noticed that there are at least three types of Christians. There are those who never read the Bible. They just call themselves Christians and that's it. Then there are those who read it here and there, and those who study it systematically every day. Then I began to study the Bible daily and participate in seminars and Bible study groups. That's when we met the *Greeks for Christ Ministry*.

My husband and I attended their meetings, which helped us spiritually in our walk with God, and in my personal Bible study. These meetings have made me little by little into a stronger Christian. I see God's answers to my prayers and His interventions in critical or simple issues in our family and in my personal life. For example, when my father went to be with the Lord on September 8, 1958.

I remember as if it were yesterday. I was hanging clothes on the wire my Dad had made for me a few months before. After about an hour, I looked through the kitchen

From Myth to Belief

window to check on the clothes and saw that the wire had been cut in half. Immediately I ran outside and sat to fold the clothes, when suddenly to my right, I saw the face of my father. He cast a quick look at me and immediately began to rise rapidly skywards. Then I saw a huge horse and rider with something like a helmet on his head. The rider held out his left hand to my father, grabbed him quickly, and they both flew together towards the heavens. Immediately I thought, "They are taking my dad!" I got up, walked slowly inside, and sat in the living room. Soon the phone rang. It was my father's doctor from Jefferson Hospital in Philadelphia.

"Mrs. Xanthopoulos, I am very sorry to say that your father has just died."

Then I understood! If millions of people had come to visit me and express their sympathy, it would not have given me as much comfort as the Lord gave me with what he showed me. Of course there may be Christians who do not believe in dreams or visions, or they believe they were just for the old times in the Old Testament. And I of course do not believe they have the power to save anyone, because only the blood of Jesus Christ can wash and cleanse the sins of man. I also believe what the New Testament reads in the second chapter of Acts, verse 17, "in the last days, says God, I will pour out of my Spirit on all flesh...and young men shall see visions, and old men shall dream dreams." And all signs indicate that we are in the last days.

The systematic daily study of the Bible gives me hope here on earth and certainty for the future, where in the golden city prepared for us by Christ there is no sun,

How Often Do You Read the Bible?

moon or night, because the eternal light is the "Lamb," and where also there will be no tears, pain, sorrow or death (Revelation, chapter 21). Yet it has had another great result on me. It gives me the strength to serve my fellow people who are in need. Frequent are my visits to hospitals and nursing homes, where I visit strangers, keep them company, ask them what I can do for them, reassure them that there is still hope, talk to them about the love of God and read to them words of consolation from the Bible. Many are those who pay close attention to the words of Christ spoken through my mouth and who ask me to pray together with them to God. Also frequent are my visits to prisons where I meet hard men and women who are still interested to hear about God's love. For many years I served in the choir and Sunday School of the Orthodox Church in my town.

Today, after many, many years of studying the Bible daily and a close relationship with Christ, I can say along with the psalmist (Psalm 119:47, 103) "I will (continue to) indulge in your commandments, which I love" and "How sweet are your words in my mouth, sweeter than honey!"

Havertown Pennsylvania
As I heard the story from Katerina Xanthopoulos

I'm Walkin', Folks...
It's a Miracle!

"All things work together for good to those who love God."
Romans 8:28

"Do you want to buy this Victorian house for a dollar?" I asked my micro-developer businessman friend Dimitri, as we were discussing business while passing by.

"Are you kidding? This huge house costs only a dollar?" he responded in surprise, eyes like sunny-side-up eggs.

"Well, of course not. But this Greek Church next door that owns the house grows fast and needs the space to create a parking lot. So, they will sell it for one dollar to anyone who wants to move it out of here and take it wherever he wants."

"You mean, I buy it for one dollar, then, I take it and go home. Correct?" he asked.

"You bet!" I responded.

"Hmmm... and where am I gonna take it. And what company will move it? And how much will it cost me to move it? And how am I going to set it up again?" The questions came like a downpour.

"What do I know? You are the developer, you'll find a way," I said assuredly.

"Well, let me think about it," added my friend as he

I'm Walkin', Folks...

walked around, inspecting it. And as he was leaving, lost in deep thought, one could almost see the smoke from the wheels of his brain spinning wildly.

"Great," I yelled from afar as he directed his steps toward his car. "You got a couple of months anyway till they demolish it. And what a shame for a Victorian beauty like this...."

"What? Demolish it?" he wondered aloud, stopping in the middle of the street. "Such a fantastic Victorian?"

"And what are they supposed to do? How are they gonna create a parking lot here?" I shot back.

Even deeper in thought, he turned around and got into his car.

Now, Dimitri, is a positive thinker and a doer. He owns two companies and a spacious house in an affluent suburb of the San Francisco Bay Area. He is also a family man with a beautiful wife, two lively children and three fast dogs. He owns the Greek television program in the area. His name is well respected by the entire Greek community throughout the region.

At that particular time, Dimitri happened to meet Dino, an experienced race horse trainer, who persuaded him to buy a young, cute racehorse. Dimitri, who had no idea about racehorses, did not want to buy the whole horse. He found a friend who had a passion for horses. The two became partners, buying him together.

There are horses and then there are *horses*. Some are proud white horses in the field you are pleased to admire. There are also some black stallions that take your breath the moment they spring to race. Dimitri's horse, however, did not resemble any of these exquisite four-legged

From Myth to Belief

beauties. He was rather skinny and his unusual pale color (something like gold) made him look even sickly. He was also wild, nervous and unpredictable. Naturally they hired Dino to train him. Dino started the horse training and Dimitri and his business partner went back to work.

Along with other businesses, Dimitri thought about the Victorian again and again. He made a lot of phone calls to city departments to learn details. He remembered of a fellow Greek who bugged him to buy a tangled plot of his about a mile away from the current position of the Victorian for a good price. He found companies specializing in moving houses. He put down the numbers. He saw that the deal was sound. So the transfer ceremony was arranged for a Sunday morning service.

An exuberant Dimitri presented a whole one dollar to the Pastor of the Church, which was accepted by him and the congregation with relief, as the developer had saved them from the demolition process and expenses. The very next day, work began for the removal of the Victorian.

Moving a house is no small task. Once one obtains multiple licenses from the municipality of the city after a lot of leg work and red tape, one has to buy hefty insurance. Then, a special work crew arrives at the site, cuts the house horizontally at its base, just above its foundations. If the height of the house is higher than the street electric or telephone wires, then the crew must also cut the roof horizontally, which happened with the Victorian. Then, towering cranes lift and place the house or whatever is left of it on a huge rectangular truck platform. The rest of the house, the roof that is, has already been placed on the platform, so the whole house is ready to move immediately.

I'm Walkin', Folks...

Moving the house started with the platform truck traveling the one mile distance at one mile per hour. Police on motorcycles and patrol cars had blocked off the streets beforehand. Electrical and telephone company trucks went just ahead of it with their crews lifting the wires using long rods so that the house would be able to pass underneath. People had gathered to watch the unusual sight. Many took videos and pictures. Without any incident, the hundred year old Victorian house arrived safe and sound at the predetermined plot, which had been prepared with foundations to accept it. Towering cranes slowly placed it exactly on the foundations. The roof was also placed on top of it. Then it was beautifully repaired, and so the house changed neighborhoods.

Meanwhile, Dino had a big problem with Dimitri's horse, because the animal was young and as all youngsters, he was totally crazy. He did not want to learn anything at all, resisting any and all the trainer's instructions. Stubbornly he ran all over the place and never to the direction the trainer wanted. Dino, an experienced race horse trainer, was now helpless. Many a times he wished he had never talked Dimitri into buying this useless animal. But he kept training him. After some time, when Dino was convinced there was nothing else the horse would learn, he proposed to the owners to take the horse to the Golden Gate Fields Racetrack in El Cerrito in the eastern San Francisco Bay and to put him to run on regular race events. He prepared them for possible failure too.

"Well, it is the first time for the horse at the track," he told them. "At least it'll be a good experience". They agreed. He found a young jockey of extra small size who

From Myth to Belief

had just arrived in the Bay Area from New York, seeking an opportunity to show he was great. The date of the race was set and all three of them, the trainer and the owners, looked forward to the big day.

Dimitri, however, had other things on his mind. The Archaeological Department insisted that the Victorian house be restored to exactly its original form, inside and out, except painted colorfully, as befits a Victorian. The restoration, however, required several changes to streamline the home according to current building code safety standards. On the one hand, crews were making the changes required by the building codes. On the other hand, the Archaeological Department arrived, ordering changes, to rebuild as they were before. Dimitri ran from department to department to straighten out every little detail of the house.

This procedure, other than the psychological damage, had economic loss. Dimitri had gotten into a sea of red, in debt, so much in fact, that he contemplated abandoning the project. However, he had to finish the house, sell it, and at least get the money he invested back. Eventually he realized he needed $50,000 to finish it, money he did not have, and he did not know where to find it. The beautiful Victorian had turned into a big nightmare. He could not sleep, eat properly or concentrate on matters of importance. At night, he would fall onto his bed with depression and unanswered questions on how he was going to get out of this predicament. In the mornings, he hated to get out of bed to go out and face the world.

"Oh my God, where do I find so much money?" Dimitri said in his prayers.

I'm Walkin', Folks...

Without realizing it, the day of the race arrived, and Dimitri went only halfheartedly to the G.G. Fields. He was not interested at all, as a matter of fact. He went alone with Dino because his partner had to suddenly travel to another city on business. When they arrived, Dimitri looked around. There were a lot of people in line to bet, bookies on the phones, lots of commotion. The G.G. Fields was alive with excitement. He looked at the display board. His horse was next to the last, with sixty to one odds of winning. His heart sank. He approached the lines at the windows. No one was betting on his horse. No one was even talking about his horse. He asked some gamblers. They looked at him puzzled and dismissed him and his horse. Dimitri went to a corner and almost cried. He thought for a moment that he had made a big mistake to get into something he did not know anything about. He was discouraged and disappointed. He even considered leaving the Fields but he couldn't because he'd given a ride to Dino. Then he turned around.

"If no one bets on my horse, I will," he thought. "He's mine after all, and if I don't support him, who will? Even if it is only for good luck, I must bet on my horse." He got in line as he put his hand into his pocket. Now, as he waited he was contemplating about how much to bet. "Twenty dollars is too cheap. Fifty. Yes, fifty is fine to bet on a horse. Well, no, fifty is too low for *my* horse. That's it, one hundred. Yes, yes, one hundred. My horse is worth at least one hundred bucks. *At least* one 100 bucks, certainly much more than $100 — *much, much more...*" At that moment, he reached the window.

He filled the ticket quickly. For some reason he couldn't

From Myth to Belief

explain, he wrote down $1,000 instead of $100 (no, it was not a mistake) and gave it to the man at the window. The man smiled when he saw that much money bet on an unknown horse, but he asked Dimitri politely,

"The ticket is incomplete. You've left the combination blank. Which other two horses do you want to bet on with this money?" Dimitri scratched his head in total confusion and marked two more horses with his eyes closed.

The race was going to start soon. The favorite, a strong brown horse, was number one. A black stallion, number three, looked anxious next to Dimitri's horse. In the middle of the two, Dimitri's sickly looking pale horse (number two) looked as though he was accidentally placed there, brought in from a farm cooperative. Everyone was shouting about his favorite horse. Dino and Dimitri sat quietly next to each other.

With the opening of the doors, the favorite horse sprang forth to the left with lightning speed, dropped off his jockey violently, returned to his line, and continued running like mad. Pandemonium in the bleachers! Most of the horses seemed to run all together, but two were way ahead, and one was way behind. Number two was just behind the latter. Dino was stone-faced, like a Babylonian statue, watching only with the professional eye of the expert trainer. Dimitri hid his face in his hands so he wouldn't have to witness the disaster.

The announcer went wild when the favorite horse fell out of competition, and he continued announcing the horses as they passed each another. Horse number two was helplessly last. Some fifty yards to go and Dimitri's horse finally opened and passed the one in front of him.

I'm Walkin', Folks...

He chased the main body of the horses running in the middle and passed them on the outside like a runaway. The throat of the speaker came out his ears as he screamed about the magnificent advance of the outsider number two, as if everything else seemed of secondary importance in the G.G. Fields. Dino sat at the edge of his seat and followed the sprint open-mouthed. He hit Dimitri hard with his elbow. Dimitri opened his eyes through his fingers in disbelief. Only a few seconds remained. Horse number two wedged himself swiftly between the other two horses and passed them like a sudden wind, finishing first, just inches ahead of the second. Dino's was jumping for joy. Dimitri was speechless, exactly like the rest of the spectators in the vastly quiet Golden Gate Fields. Only the P.A. system blurred the voice of the announcer:

"I'm Walkin'" (this was the name of Dimitri's horse), "I'm Walkin', folks... I'm Walkin' has finished first. Incredible!"

Dimitri's hand went to the pocket. Did he still have the ticket? He pulled it out of his pocket, wanting to make sure he had it right. Yes, he marked his horse first. Then he realized he had also marked the other two horses second and third exactly as they had finished. He almost fainted. Suddenly the flashing cameras of the reporters brought him back to reality as they came to take pictures of the horse, to interview the jockey, him and Dino. All of a sudden Dimitri was circled by some important people. Somehow, he became important himself. They took him to the winner's circle lounge to collect. When the amount was announced to him, he really did faint: $100,000. Who wouldn't?

On the way back home, Dimitri caressed the $100,000

From Myth to Belief

check in his pocket, money he did not have a couple of hours before when they drove to the G.G. Fields. The fifty grand was his. And then suddenly, the light went on. He had exactly the amount he needed to finish his Victorian house! Was that a miracle or what?

Golden Gate Fields, El Cerrito - Oakland California
As I heard the story from Dimitri Karapanos

Note: According to Mr. Karapanos his horse "I'm Walkin'" never made any good appearance after this in any race and he was sold shortly thereafter. The Victorian house was completed with this money and was sold, making him a good profit.

A Miracle Like No Other...

There is no award without a struggle.
Struggles without award are many.

Bob is one of the best missionaries I have ever met. He is happy when he gives, and he's so humble that when they would honor him for anything, he'd return the honor in practical terms.

From an early age he wanted to be a missionary, to travel to the wild places of Africa, to find the natives and tell them the greatest love story ever, that of God, which was revealed to people in order to save them from their sins. He knew that this would not only make them happy, but it would improve their everyday lives too.

He married a beautiful girl, Rebecca, who also had the same desire in her heart. They went to college together to prepare, worked hard to save for their fares and expenses for four years in Africa, and then left for Senegal when they were about twenty-five years old.

All things in Africa were as strange as they expected them and perhaps even stranger. As soon as they arrived, they crisscrossed the jungles amidst a thousand dangers in order to find people to tell them about their love of God. The natives had never heard such things and accepted them with kindness. The minute the chieftain of the Sereres tribe saw Bob, he fell on his knees bowing, in front of him and saying,

From Myth to Belief

"The Great Spirit brought you in my sleep last night. I was expecting you."

The chieftain gathered the whole tribe to welcome the guests and hear what they had to say. Immediately Bob and Becky grabbed the opportunity to preach of the true and living God who loved them and sent for them his only son Jesus Christ. The natives had never heard about a God of love. Their gods were spirits that quite often had to be appeased through special rituals and certain sacrifices because they were always very unhappy, if not angry, with the people of their tribe. Bob continued preaching about Jesus who loves the world, heals the people, and teaches them to respect and love one another. He even told them that because all people are sinners, Jesus willingly died in their place so that we sinners will not die for our sins. He told them that this Jesus also rose from the dead, ascended into heaven and is now in the right side of the Father, and that no one who now accepts him will die. Furthermore, Jesus makes a new man of him by giving him strength to love his fellow man and to live harmoniously with everyone.

The natives received the Word of God and praised the Lord Jesus Christ who loved them. All were thrilled and delighted with the missionary and his preaching. That is, all except the voodoo master of the tribe who was losing his job to missionary Bob. When darkness fell that evening, everyone left quickly to their huts to sleep (as is usual in the jungle). As Bob and Becky went to their makeshift tent, they thanked God that they found grace in front of the natives. They opened a can of spam and crackers from their supplies, ate dinner, and prayed for everyone, even the tribe voodoo master, that the Lord would soften his

A Miracle Like No Other...

heart. With that, they slipped into their sleeping bag in a loving embrace.

The next day, the missionaries showed the natives how to make many household things. They took the chieftain, the voodoo master and other tribe dignitaries for a ride in their little jeep, and in the afternoon they held a meeting again. Becky played the portable little battery harmonica that she always carried with her while her husband sang a few hymns. The natives went crazy over the singing box. At the end of the meeting, the chieftain got up and announced with enthusiasm,

"We will have a great gathering on Sunday. We will celebrate that God sent us the missionaries. We will hear what they have to say, we will sing together and then we'll have a big banquet, the whole tribe."

Bob and Becky could not believe the effect the Word of God had in the hearts and lives of these simple natives. They thanked the Lord for his blessings. And they ate their carefully rationed canned supplies each day.

From that Thursday until the following Sunday, everyone in the village went crazy over the preparations, working feverishly. Some went hunting, others were building a grandstand (under Bob's instructions of course). Others cut wood or dug. The women carried things, and the children ran all over doing nothing. The big day arrived and everything was festive. The chieftain had worn all his feathers; all his women adorned themselves proudly with colorful robes, which were in fact bed-sheets Becky gave them. The tribal officials all wore something that the missionaries had given them as a gift. One had a pair of sunglasses on, another a tie, someone a leather belt,

From Myth to Belief

another hat, someone else socks, another one shoes, someone underwear, another one a T-shirt, someone a jacket, and one young man a pair of blue jeans. Other than this, everyone was naked.

The meeting took place as planned. The missionaries preached about Christ and taught the crowd many hymns. When the service was over, they all sat at the big banquet. Bob as the honored guest sat next to the chieftain, Becky next to Bob, and the voodoo master sat on the other side of the chieftain. The chefs and the servers came and went bringing platters of roasts and assorted other hearty dishes that Bob and Becky had never seen in their lives.

They wondered with alarm what kind of meat and greens were before them, and if it was safe to eat. The mere thought of their canned food made their mouths water. It was perhaps the first time in their lives that they would pass up freshly prepared food for canned food. "Oh, I wish I had a spam now..." Bob thought.

"I want just crackers. Nothing else..." whispered Becky to herself.

The voodoo master caught the concerns of the missionaries and advised the chieftain whispering in his ear:

"Offer the missionary a piece of meat. If he eats it, he's really genuine. If he offends you by not taking the meat, kill him immediately so he will not spoil our tradition."

The chieftain rose, speaking the highest praises about Bob, saying that he was god-sent, that he was the best man he had ever met, and that he was wise and knew everything. "And as guest of honor," the chieftain continued, "I offer him the best gift in our tradition, the best

A Miracle Like No Other...

part of the roast." He turned and offered him the largest platter. Bob lowered his eyes and along with the platter he received the surprise of his life: the head of a monkey, cooked and garnished expertly, gazing at him. Bob turned and looked at his wife, but found no help. She could only look at him in horror.

Bob contemplated his next move. He had to think of something fast, even while he was still standing. Everyone was seated except the chieftain and Bob. Bob was still holding the platter. He raised his eyes imploringly to heaven, as if he was saying grace before dinner. All eyes were riveted on Bob. You could hear a pin drop. It was like the treacherous calm before a thunderstorm. It was as if the voodoo master had broadcasted all his hatred of the missionaries to each member of the tribe by telepathy. They all felt that something terrible was going to happen, something all would participate in. The voodoo master gripped his knife, ready for action.

Bob with platter in hands lowered his eyes slowly, looked around the seated crowd, took a deep breath, and said, still smiling,

"I thank the Most Merciful God for this moment. In addition, I thank the Honorable chieftain for the honor he has bestowed upon my wife Becky and me. I would accept this unique gift if I were the most important person in this meeting. However, right after Christ, the most prominent person in this gathering here is and will always be the great King-Chieftain. To him belongs the best part of the meat, because without him, we would not be here." So, he turned around and offered the platter back to the chieftain.

The crowd erupted in cheers, clapping, chanting, and

From Myth to Belief

dancing. The chieftain could not keep his emotions in check. He embraced Bob, perhaps showing public affection for the first time judging by how confused his subjects looked for a moment before continuing the celebration with greater intensity. Becky, in tears, took a deep breath of relief. And the voodoo master got up at that very moment and left. To this day, no one knows where he vanished.

Since then, Bob and Becky were like gods among the Sereres tribe. They stayed with them all four years of their stay in Africa. They even used this area as their headquarters when visiting other tribes in the jungle. They continued preaching the love of God to everyone. When they finally did return to their homeland, many tribes had accepted Christ and they were all on their way to civilization with buildings, schools, and arts to show for it. They were so successful that the Chief of Police told Bob in his farewell, "If there others like you in America please send them over here to help our people."

Senegal; New Brockton, Alabama; Oakland, California
As I heard the story from the Rev. Robert Creel

Which Religion is the Best?

> *An awesome greatness is inherent in the stillness of the Middle East. Unlike what happens in the Western world, God here speaks deep inside within you with a soft, gentle voice.*

Being born a Christian! I would be expected to say that Christianity is the best religion, but the answer to this question was not given to me at birth. I had to travel many miles to find the correct answer myself. This story is an account of my much-desired and long-planned trip to the Holy Land, the birthplace of three of the main religions of the world, and the holy ground where I anticipated to meet God.

I grew up in another holy land, called Greece. This is where my great, great grandpa, Homer, many, many centuries ago deified man, rather the Greek man and woman, elevating them to Mt. Olympus. In my younger years, I played soccer at the foot of Mars Hill and regularly, almost religiously, visited the Parthenon, the temple of the goddess of wisdom, the virgin Athena, which was converted in the 5th century AD into a Christian church dedicated to another virgin, the mother of Jesus, Virgin Mary. Therefore, I was somewhat familiar with holy stuff.

A burning desire, however, was growing inside of me to visit the Holy Land someday. For years, I prepared myself by studying the Torah, the Mosaic Law and the rest of the

From Myth to Belief

Old Testament, the New Testament, the Koran, and holy books of other religions.

I also studied ancient and contemporary maps and any related articles I found from time to time in newspapers and magazines.

At last, on one bright summer day I boarded the plane with great expectations to visit the holiest place of the Jewish, Christian, and Muslim faiths. My excitement ran wild, even as "a wisdom seeking Greek," knowing that shortly I would be setting foot on the Holy Land.

I wanted to see what was so special about the city called Jerusalem that countless mighty armies conquered and then lost. I was thrilled to be able to hear the muse that inspired King David, St. John, and Prophet Muhammad. I was eager, prayerfully so, to hear the voice of the Almighty; perhaps, not in that dramatic way as He spoke to these great men, but at least in some small way in my little heart. I just desired to connect. I was fully prepared for the experience that would change my life. Even if it did not, it at least would leave an indelible stamp in the depths of my being.

As soon as I landed, I dropped off my luggage at a five star hotel and then I was off to mingle with the people downtown. I felt really at home, exactly like I was in my hometown of Athens, Greece. The streets were narrow, the buses slow moving, the buildings were Mediterranean style, the people were svelte and nervous, even their noses looked like the Greeks'.

First, I visited the site of the Holy Sepulcher. The pilgrimage up narrow Via Dolorosa reminded me of the moneychangers, the buyers, and the sellers at the Temple

Which Religion is the Best?

in the time of Jesus. Only Christ casting them out was missing. A few more short steps and I reached the top of the hill, where the tomb of Jesus is supposed to be located. There I realized there are three sites for the tomb.

Well, actually, it is just one, but it depends from which side you are facing. One side is the (Greek) Eastern Orthodox; another is the Armenian Apostolic, and finally the Roman Catholic. Certainly, you leave a monetary offering at the side you visit to worship. The Greek side I visited first, though it had the longest line. When I spoke to the Greek Orthodox priest in Greek he got so excited hearing his native tongue that he led me by the hand straight to the head of the line. I was so moved then that I left even a greater donation in his blessed hand. Leaving it, I circled the famous tomb so I could at least see the other sides of it from afar. Then I headed to the garden of Gethsemane, where the actual tomb carved into the rock lays according to the Protestants. Those shameless capitalists issued tickets! Something stung me in the heart as I walked down to the Wailing Wall.

When I arrived, reverent Rabbis stopped me at the gate, for I did not wear a hat. They handed me one that looked like a McDonald's large-order French fries paper cup, because, they told me, the great Jehovah does not look favorably upon men uncovered. I entered the sacred court of the Wall and I noticed that the place was divided in two by a chicken-wire fence the height of some three feet. On this side, the men prayed to Jehovah; on the other side, the women did. "Do the women pray to their own Jehovah?" I wondered. All black-clothed rabbis, old and young men and children, faced the wall and read prayers

From Myth to Belief

from little black books while swinging their body back and forth. Right then I looked around and got the surprise of my life. Leaning lazily on the Wall was a group of young priests nonchalantly talking on their cellular phones. "Aha," I thought, "now these priests are really up-to-date, talking to Jehovah in a way I understand." I left the Wall behind for the gold-leaf covered Mosque of Omar, deep in thought.

There young reverent Imams commanded me to take off my shoes, because, they carefully explained, Allah does not hear people in shoes. When I entered, the mosque was empty of people, because it was not the time of prayer for the faithful. Ahead of me, however, stretched wall-to-wall, were the most beautiful colorful silk carpets I've ever seen in my life. They seemed so preciously wonderful pieces of art to me that taking off the shoes seemed reasonable. And in the very front of the Mosque, elderly reverent Imams sat cross-legged on the carpeted floor praying or having a holy discussion, I do not know, while counting beads or playing their huge 'komboloi,' or worry beads in their hand. Still deep in thought, I headed to a Christian church.

There again I was stopped, because the Christian God, they stressed to me, is not pleased to see men in shorts and women in mini-skirts in his church. Fortunately, the reverent, elderly, farseeing priest had foreseen for some trousers and dresses to hang on the branches of a tree in the churchyard, so he lent me a pair of trousers. As I was putting it on a large group of Scandinavian tourists arrived. However, there were not enough trousers for all of the men in the group. The black-robed priest scratched his long-bearded jaw and handed a dress to a tall, skinny,

Which Religion is the Best?

school, at work or in the countryside, in my car, on the train, or in an airplane, even in my private room. He covers me in any way I present myself humbly in front of him.

Well, I had to go to the Holy Land to understand that there was no need to go to the Holy Land to meet God!

Oakland, California, Holy Land, Greek Islands